the BUZZ

★"**WICKEDLY FUNNY** and **ICONOCLASTIC.** This is no litany of Zen orthodoxy designed for study. **ENTERTAINING,** bold and **REFRESHINGLY DIRECT,** this book is likely to change the way one experiences other books about Zen—and maybe even the way one experiences reality."
Publishers Weekly (starred review)
also a PW selection for "The Year in Books"

"**WARNER IS ONE OF US.** When he talks about Zen, it's with a bluntness and **ACIDIC SENSE OF HUMOR** that belongs to us as well. Most importantly, he presents it in honest, **DOWN-TO-EARTH** language that shows how these ideas connect to our immediate lives."
Maximumrocknroll

"Capable of **DEVASTATING HUMOR;** Warner **PULLS NO PUNCHES.** His book is an honest account of his search for **TRUTH.**"
Booklist

"You **NEED** to **READ THIS BOOK.**"
Bill Stevenson,
member of punk bands All, The Descendents, and Black Flag

"**GONZO,** and often **HILARIOUS.**"
Dharmalife

"**MAN OH MAN,** this is a **VERY** GOOD book."
Janwillem van de Wetering,
author of The Empty Mirror and
The Corpse on the Dike

the AUTHOR

BRAD WARNER was a kid from the town of **WADSWORTH, OHIO,** who managed to get himself to the **CUTTING EDGE** of the **HARDCORE PUNK** scene in  the early '80s. He played bass for **ZERO DEFEX,** one of the noisiest of the hardcore punk bands, and recorded five albums under the band name **DIMENTIA 13.** He eventually found himself in Japan, working on low-budget **GODZILLA-TYPE MOVIES** and **ULTRAMAN** television shows, all the while studying with a **ZEN MASTER.** Now that same hardcore punk is also a Zen priest. But he's **NOT ABOUT TO SAY THAT HIS PUNK DAYS ARE OVER** now that he's "seen the light"—far from it. Warner's equally at home in a **LOUD BASEMENT CLUB** or a **REMOTE ZEN TEMPLE.** When not at his day job, Brad Warner teaches **HARDCORE ZEN** in lectures and meditation retreats in and around **TOKYO.**

more BUZZ

"This is ZEN FOR THE SOUTH PARK SET: SUBVERSIVE,
shit-stick dharma liberally laced with scenes
from Warner's life [which] will no doubt RESONATE.
Hardcore Zen is Be Here Now for now."
Tricycle: The Buddhist Review

"Readers are likely to finish Hardcore Zen
with a wider understanding of the
VAST ARRAY OF HUMAN SPIRITUAL IDEALS."
Foreword

"DOWN-TO-EARTH and FUNNY. It's rare to encounter
someone who can claim authority on such a
wide variety of the USELESS and PROFOUND, but
Warner has the résumé to back it up. He sees
Buddhism as a TRUTH-SEEKING METHOD, a means of
CONFRONTING REALITY. Hardcore Zen will probably
make you reconsider how you spend your time."
CityBeat

"I like this book!—ripping & snorting in all
directions....grabbing a FISTFUL OF PUNK ROCK, a
SNOUTFUL OF POPULAR CULTURE, & more than a HANDFUL OF
MOVIE MOMENTS—all of 'em pitched into a spinning,
full-tilt Zen blender. THE DAMN THING MAKES SENSE!"
Bill Shields, author of
The Southeast Asian Book of the Dead

"Hardcore Zen deftly links punk idealism,
POP CULTURE and a SPIRITUAL QUEST in a way
that seems at once surprising and obvious. This
is the sound of ONE HAND THRASHING!"
David Giffels & Jade Dillinger, authors of
Are We Not Men? We Are DEVO!

and still MORE buzz

"This is the REAL DEAL."
James Ishmael Ford,
Head Teacher of Boundless Way Zen
and author of This Very Moment

"I've always had an interest in Eastern thought
but was put off by the placid lake-and-lotus-blos-
som tone of everything I'd read. It's nice to know
that PUNK ROCK AND ZEN AREN'T IRRECONCILABLE AFTER ALL."
Jeff Hagedorn, Owned & Operated Recordings

"I never thought that any book could fit in
Klaus Nomi, Ultraman and a description of a
practical theology but Brad Warner has done it.
It's A GREAT F***ING BOOK, read it and then do
as the BAD BRAINS commanded us and DESTROY BABYLON."
Rev. Hank Peirce, Parish Minister,
Unitarian Universalist Church of Medford (Mass.)

"It's nice to read something that actually makes
you think and laugh—there were times I LAUGHED SO HARD I
COULDN'T BREATHE. This book KICKS ASS. Damn good job."
Jennifer Martin, The Book Merchant
(Natchitoches, Louisiana)

HARDCORE ZEN

HARDCORE ZEN

PUNK ROCK
monster movies
& the
TRUTH ABOUT
reality

BRAD WARNER

Wisdom Publications • Boston

Wisdom Publications
199 Elm Street
Somerville MA 02144 USA
www.wisdompubs.org

Library of Congress Cataloging-in-Publication Data
Warner, Brad.
    Hardcore Zen : punk rock, monster movies and the truth about
reality / Brad Warner.
        p. cm.
    ISBN 0-86171-380-X (pbk. : alk paper)
    1. Spiritual life—Zen Buddhism. 2. Warner, Brad. 3. Spiritual
biography—United States. 4. Spiritual biography—Japan. I. Title.
    BQ9288.W37 2003
    294.3'927—dc21

                                                    2003011829

07 06 05 04
5   4   3   2

Cover by Elizabeth Lawrence
Interior by Elizabeth Lawrence and Gopa & Ted2

Toilet used by permission of Someday Cafe, Davis Square, Somerville.
Illustrations on page 187–189 by Andrew Campbell
Author photo by Takeshi Yagi

Wisdom Publications' books are printed on acid-free paper and
meet the guidelines for permanence and durability of the
Committee on Production Guidelines for Book Longevity of the
Council on Library Resources.

Printed in the United States of America

I have no time for lies or fantasy
and neither should you.
Enjoy or die.

JOHN LYDON, aka JOHNNY ROTTEN
FROM *ROTTEN*

CONTENTS

PROLOGUE

For me it was this: Turning away from an overflowing toilet in a crummy basement bar in the middle of an Ohio winter with a bunch of apes in leather jackets outside shouting in unison as some other ape in a pair of stretch-pants thrashes away at an imitation Les Paul guitar running through a busted Marshall amp. The lights, the noise, the girl by the bar in the sweaty white T-shirt that I can just about see through... All of a sudden I'm struck with the senselessness, the absurdity, the sheer overwhelming weirdness of it all.

What is this place? This existence—the very fact of my being—what is this? Who am I? What is this thing, this body, its ears ringing from the noise, its eyes burning from the smoke, its stomach churning from the pissy-tasting swill that passes for beer?

IT ALL CAME TO A HEAD that night but those have always been the kinds of burning questions that bit into the core of my being since I was old enough to think. Not questions like, "What is the purpose of existence? What is the meaning of life? Where did we come from?"—those were always too indirect for me. Meaning is removed from real existence. Purpose deals with goals, direction, and stuff that's going to happen in the future. Wherever we came from is over and done. That doesn't get at it for me. It doesn't get right at the root of things. I want to know what *this* is—this place right here, this state of mind right now. *What is this?*

Or to put it another way: What is truth itself? What is this thing called reality?

NOW, AFTER YEARS AND YEARS of intense questioning I feel like I have something to say—and more than that, I feel I almost have a duty to say it.

Why should you listen to me? Who the hell am I? Who is this guy who's claiming he's gonna give you the skinny on "the truth about reality" as if he's an authority? No one. No one at all.

The fact is, although I can tell you who I am and what I've done, I can't give you any real reasons why you ought to listen to me. There aren't any reasons. It's not about reasons.

For the record, I'll tell you I'm an ordained Buddhist priest who received *Shiho*, "Dharma Transmission," in an ancient line of Buddhist teachers. This is supposedly the symbolic recognition that I have "attained" the same enlightenment as the Buddha did some 2,500 years ago— but if I were you I wouldn't put too much stock in that kind of thing. Guys who've received Dharma Transmission are a dime a dozen here in Japan these days, and there are scores of them in America and Europe as well. Big deal.

Before I was a Buddhist priest I was a part of the early hardcore punk and alternative music scene. I played bass in Zero Defex, an Ohio hardcore punk band whose only significant recorded release was the song "Drop the A-Bomb on Me" on a compilation called *P.E.A.C.E./ War.* * This double album, on which the Dead Kennedys, the Butthole Surfers, MDC, and a host of other hardcore legends appeared, has been reissued numerous times over the past

----

*I'd like to mention, for the benefit of the good folks at that record label that I'm still waiting for my royalties.

twenty years and because of it our little band is far more well known now than it was when we were playing. I cut a deal with New York's Midnight Records label and released five albums of Syd Barrett–influenced neo-psychedelia under the band name Dimentia 13 (though on three of those records the "band" consisted of me alone). Those records sold well enough and influenced enough people to earn me the everlasting recognition of my own little footnote in the history of alternative rock—if you own the right coupla books.

As far as earning a living now, I'm in the prestigious line of making B-grade Japanese monster movies. You know the kind: two out-of-work sumo wrestlers dress up in rubber dinosaur costumes and slam the bejeezus out of each other on a scale model of Tokyo made out of balsa wood and model train kits. The company I work for was founded by the late, great Mr. Eiji Tsuburaya, the man who directed the special effects for all of the classic Godzilla movies of the '50s and '60s. These days we make a show called *Ultraman*, which is perhaps the single most popular superhero character throughout half the world—although if you live in the America half, you might never have heard of him.

None of this makes me inherently worth listening to—as I'm sure you'll be quick to agree. Yet truth is truth. And if words are true, who cares whether the guy who wrote them has *Shiho* or Divine Inspiration or the power to fly faster than a speeding bullet?

So, if you're interested in what I have to say, keep reading. If you find something, some little thing that resonates and might do some good in your life, great. If you get to the end of this book (or to the middle, or to page 27 second paragraph down) and think the book is crap, leave it on the subway and forget about it. No problem.

But before you do, ask yourself just one thing:
Who are you?

I'm not talking about your name, your job, or the number of hairs on your butt. Who the hell are you *really*? And what really is that thing you so confidently call your life?

GIMME SOME TRUTH

Sometimes the truth hurts.
And sometimes it feels real good.
HENRY ROLLINS

NOTHING IS SACRED. Doubt—in everything—is absolutely
essential. Everything, no matter how great, how fundamental, how beautiful, or important it is, must be questioned.

It's only when people believe that their beliefs are above questioning, that their beliefs alone are beyond all doubt, that they can be as truly horrible as we all know they can be. Belief is the force behind every evil mankind has ever done. You can't find one truly evil act in human history that was not based on belief—and the stronger their belief, the more evil human beings can be.

Here's one of *my* beliefs: Everything is sacred. Every blade of grass, every cockroach, every speck of dust, every flower, every pool of mud outside a graffiti-splattered warehouse is God. Everything is a worthy object of worship. If you can't bow down before that putrefying roadkill on I-76, you have no business worshiping leatherbound tomes and marble icons surrounded by stained glass.

And here's one more: Everything is profane. "Saving the planet" is a waste of time and preserving the environment is a waste of energy. Flowers stink and birdsong is irritating noise.

On the other hand, *nothing* is sacred and *nothing* is profane. Not even your sorry ass. If we hold anything sacred above anything else—ever—we're riding along in the fast-lane to hell. And by "anything" I mean *anything*—our family, our friends, our country, our God. We cannot hold any of that stuff any more sacred than anything else we encounter in our lives or we're doomed. I'm not just going for dramatic elocution here. The act of regarding *anything at all* as more worthy of respect than anything else is the first step down the short and slippery path to the utter annihilation of all mankind.

And what happens if we follow that dangerous path to the end? We've had numerous hints that ought to give us a clue. They linger darkly on in our collective memories: the assassinations of Martin Luther King Jr. and John F. Kennedy, the bombing of Pearl Harbor, the atomic bombings of Hiroshima and Nagasaki, the Final Solution, "9-11." We might even be able to rattle off the dates of these awful events—but the lesson, we haven't yet absorbed. And until we really learn it, kids will keep getting new dates to memorize for history class.

When you hold something sacred, you try to hold that thing apart from the rest of the universe. But this really can't be done. Nothing can be separated from everything else. Red is only red because it's not green or yellow or blue. Heavy metal is heavy metal because it's not polka or barbershop. Nothing in the universe has any inherent existence apart from everything else. Good is only good when contrasted with evil. You are only you because you're not everyone else. But this kind of separateness isn't really how the universe works.

You cannot possibly honor God if you can't honor every last one of God's manifestations. Killing someone in God's name is ridiculous. If we do that, we are killing God and killing truth.

But what is truth? What is God? How can you see, hear, smell, taste, touch, these lofty ideas?

Truth screams at you from billboard cigarette ads. God sings to you in Muzak® versions of Barry Manilow songs. Truth announces itself when you kick away a discarded bottle of Colt 45 Malt Liquor. Truth rains on you from the sky above, and God forms in puddles at your feet. You eat God and excrete truth four hours later. Take a whiff—what a lovely fragrance the truth has! Truth is reality itself. God is reality itself. Enlightenment, by the way, is reality itself. And here it is.

And just FYI: Even if you run and run and run forever you can't possibly escape reality. You can fervently deny the existence of an Ultimate Truth or of God, but reality is always right there staring you in the face. And you can search and search for enlightenment, but you'll only ever find reality.

You won't find enlightenment by eating 'shrooms or smoking some really primo weed. And enlightenment's not in books. Not even this one.

Some people think enlightenment is some kind of superspecial state without questions or doubts, some kind of absolute faith in your beliefs and the rightness of your perceptions. That's not enlightenment. In fact, that's the very worst kind of delusion. And just so we're clear from the get-go, let me state for the record that I have not "attained enlightenment." Never have and never will. And yet, there is *something*, and even though this experience doesn't change anything at all, it changes everything.

To "know" that what you believe is absolutely 100 percent now-and-forever utterly and completely True is the sickest, most vile, and most foul perversion of everything worthwhile in humanity, of all that is right in the world. Truth can never be found in mere belief. Belief is restricted. Truth is boundless.

Truth doesn't screw around, and truth doesn't care about your opinions. It doesn't care if you believe in it, deny it, or ignore it. It couldn't care less what religion you are, what country you're from, what color your skin is, what or who you've got between your legs, or how much you've got invested in Mutual Funds. None of the trivial junk that concerns most people most of the time matters even one teensy-weensy bit to the truth.

Oh, and one other thing: The truth is not open to negotiation—not by you, not by me, and not by the Leader of the Free World or the Moral Majority. The truth simply *is*.

THE WORLD IS IN DEEP SHIT RIGHT NOW. The only thing that can possibly save us from our own self-induced destruction is direct knowledge of the truth. And I say that without any reservation at all. Mankind cannot survive unless the truth dawns—from within—in each and every one of us. No political solution, bellicose *or* peaceful, will ever save us. No law. No pact. No treaty. No war.

We have developed the capacity to destroy ourselves and each other utterly and that is never going to go away. All we can do now is develop the capacity to see that we must never use that power—and we must see this not just individually but collectively, as the human race itself, as *life* itself, and from the very core of our collective being.

The lame-ass "solutions" we hear from political leaders, windbag pontificators, preachers, warmongers, peaceniks, tree-huggers, Bible-thumpers—without the clarity of truth behind them, they're all meaningless, yammering noise. Trying to understand their twaddle makes about as much sense as trying to interpret the screeching of Lou Reed's *Metal Machine Music* as a subtle treatise on the nature of being.

These talking heads are all trying to take truth and force it into categories of their own design. It's as if they're scooping up a bucketful of ocean water and saying that now that they've got it neatly in a bucket they totally understand what the sea really is. *Right.*

Before we can meaningfully talk about any of this, we need to address the real questions: What *is* all this? Who am I? Who are you? Why are we suffering?

Personally, I've never been interested in sugar-coated imitations of truth, sweet little pseudo-truth pills I could take three times a day with meals and a beer chaser. And to me, this seems at best to be what all religions, philosophies, and political views have to offer.

Religions, the supposed institutional repositories of humanity's understanding of the deeper mysteries of the universe, have never offered anything more to me than sophisticated methods of *avoiding* the truth, of building elaborate fantasies in place of reality. As far as I'm concerned, religions obscure reality rather than reveal it more clearly. They serve up vapid platitudes in place of answers to the genuine and crucial questions that burn in our guts. Pretty buildings full of vacant-eyed people with freeze-dried brains all pretending to agree with each other that the empty words the guy up front wearing the funny costume says actually mean anything at all let alone anything actually useful—that whole scene never did a lot for me. Religions offer authority figures: Trust the wise people's learned excretions and you'll be fine. Uh-huh.

And philosophy, the academically sanctioned state religion of the Western world, isn't any better. Philosophies offer clever suppositions phrased in five-dollar words. Sure, philosophy can lead to a deep-ass insight or two. Maybe you even have some orgasmically important philosophical thought and bask in its glow as you puff your self-congratulatory cigar and write it up for a journal—but soon enough you look around and the world is still the same old screwed-up mess.

Politics? Politicians can't solve the problem of how to find their own asses with two hands and a flashlight, let alone figure out anything more complex and subtle.

Fame, fortune, really great sex—maybe those'll cure all your ills. But beautiful famous people with loads of money are just as confused and miserable as anyone else. Spend your whole life chasing after wealth and power and you end up with nothing more to show for it than bleeding ulcers and a heart condition. You can master tantric yogic poly-orgasmic Wonder Sex but you're still gonna die alone. There has to be something more.

MY OWN QUEST for truth began because I knew there had to be some way to see the truth that didn't involve following all the other cattle to the slaughterhouse. There had to be some way for me to see truth clearly—without relying on anyone else to interpret the world for me. There had to be a way to cut through this mess I was living in. And to see what the hell was going on with this mess I called *me*.

In my search for something real, I discovered Zen Buddhism. Before I found out what it really was, I'd passed over Buddhism several times. Everything I ever read about Buddhism made me think it was about sitting with my legs all twisted up and vegging out while visions of pretty flowers and fluffy white clouds danced through my mind. *Yeah*, I figured, *like that's ever gonna solve anything.*

It's a damned shame that so much so-called Buddhist writing seems intended to function like spiritual elevator music. Mix up some lullaby-style writing and a few well-worn Buddhist clichés—or quotes from Yoda *("Let the Force flow through you!")* and David Carradine's character in *Kung Fu ("Patience, Grasshopper!")*, if you don't know any real Buddhist soundbites—wrap it all up in a serene cover with a ripply-water picture and—*Hey! Yer makin' Buddhism!*

I was lucky enough to meet a real Buddhist teacher (and not just a "buddhistic" poseur) at a comparatively young age. I was nineteen at the time and he was thirty-five—a little younger than I am now. The Buddhism he taught me was nothing like any of the religions or philosophies I'd read about up until then; it was something completely different.

The last thing Buddha told his followers before he died was this: "Question authority." Actually, if you look it up, you might see his last words translated as, "Be ye lamps unto yourselves." A lot of guys who translated this kind of stuff really got into the King James Bible–sounding language. But the point is, a lamp is something you use to guide yourself in the dark. "Be lamps unto yourselves" means be your own master, be your own lamp. Don't believe something because your hero, your teacher, or even Buddha himself said it. Look for yourself. *See* for yourself, with your own eyes. "Be lamps unto yourselves." It's another way of saying, "Question authority."

And here's something else unique about Zen: While Christianity teaches that man was expelled from the Garden of Eden, Zen teaches that we are living in paradise right now, even amid all the shit that's going down. This world is the Pure Land. This world is paradise. In fact, this world is *better* than paradise—but all we can do is piss and moan, and look around for something better.

But it's not just "Buddhism" or "Zen" that says that. It's me, right now to you. And I'll say it again: This world is better than paradise, better than any Utopia you can imagine. I say that in the face of war and starvation and suicide bombings and Orange Terror Alerts. This world is better than Utopia because—and follow this point carefully—*you can never live in Utopia*. Utopia is always somewhere else. That's the very definition of Utopia.

Maybe you can go to a paradisiacal island, far away from your boss and your bills and anything else you want, but pretty soon you'll be complaining that you've got sand up your ass, or the snack machine ate your dollar, or hermit crabs stole your thongs. You'll always find something wrong with wherever you are because it will *never quite match* your idea of what it "should" be.

You can't go to paradise. Not now and not after you make your first million. Not after you die. And not if you eat all your peas and are really, really good. Not ever. What you call "you" can never enter the gates of heaven, no matter how convictedly you believe. Heaven and paradise aren't in your future because you have no future. There is no future for you. There is no future for anyone. There is no future at all. Future is an idea.

You can't live in paradise—but you are living right here. Make this your paradise or make this your hell. The choice is entirely yours. Really.

So what's real Zen and how can a person who doesn't know much about Buddhism separate the real deal from the books about getting blissed-out and having weird acid-trippy experiences that certain sad, misled folk call "enlightenment"? Well, there's no easy answer to that question. But watch out for that *e*-word. Don't expect too much of it. And watch out for the people who tell you they've got it and you don't. And *especially* watch out for the people who say they can give it to you. The main rule of thumb is to use those critical thinking skills they taught you in school. Whether you have a background in Buddhist "scholarship" is entirely irrelevant. The fact is, it's hard to find a group of people who misunderstand Buddhism more thoroughly than Buddhist scholars. And often, the more renowned the scholar the more likely he's got his head firmly wedged in his ass. Question what you read and hear, question deeply and continually. Don't accept anything because other people believe it, or because it's expressed prettily or because it's been around for twenty or two hundred or two thousand years. And by all means, question *this*, too. But go all the way with your questioning: Question your own conclusions, your own judgments, and your own answers. Look at your own beliefs, your own prejudices, your own opinions—and see them for what they are.

If you don't do that, the truth can never appear. And if it doesn't appear in a way that you can personally grasp it without reservation, this whole world hasn't got a chance in hell.

But if you really thoroughly question *everything*, if you pursue your questions long enough and honestly enough, there will come a time when truth will wallop you upside the head and you will *know*.

But let me offer a warning, which like everything else I say, you are totally free to disregard: The truth won't be what you imagined. It won't even be close. And you may well wish you hadn't chased it so long. But once you find it you will never be able to run away from it again, and you will never be able to hide. You'll have no choice but to face up to it.

DORK-BOY &the GODHEAD

All of my life spent wondering who's hiding behind this face of mine.

"ORIGINAL ME" BY ALL FROM THE ALBUM BREAKING THINGS

AUTOBIOGRAPHIES SUCK. It's so easy for them to become self-centered, self-absorbed exercises in self-importance. And besides that, autobiographies inevitably promote the very un-Buddhist view that human beings are individual entities acting autonomously from the rest of the universe. That's crap. You only *think* you have a mind of your own, buddy. Ain't no such thing.

But sometimes some autobiographical details have their place in a bigger picture, so I'm gonna share a few with you here. How about if I start with a heartwarming little story about a spiritual master I once knew?

BACK IN THE EARLY '80s, I was yer typical pimply-faced college dork-boy attending my first semester at Kent State University—a campus whose dubious claim to fame was the slaughter of four students by the Ohio National Guard during a 1970 antiwar demonstration. Like lots of people my age, I was searching for a spiritual path. One day I saw a flier saying the Hare Krishnas would be holding free vegetarian cooking classes on campus. Now I'd been a fan of The Beatles since junior high and knew George Harrison

was deeply into the Hare Krishnas. And, because the foreword was written by George Harrison, I even owned a copy
of International Society for Krishna Consciousness founder
A.C. Bahaktivedanta Swami Prabhupada's book *Krishna:
The Supreme Personality of Godhead*. So I knew the story
of how Prabhupada, a poor but devout Indian monk, had
come to America in the early '60s and succeeded in winning converts all over the West to his charismatic brand of
Hindu mysticism. Beatle George had rejected Transcendental Meditation in favor of the Krishnas. So I knew I had
to check 'em out.

The guy who ran the cooking class happened to be the
head of the Hare Krishna temple in Cleveland. He was an
Anglo-type but he went by some Indian "spiritual name" I
can't recall. I do remember him telling us how this "spiritual name" was chosen by his spiritual master for its
resemblance in sound to his "karma name," which was
Terry. I was real impressed with this guy. He had the saffron
robes, the shaved head, and that mellow spiritual way of
talking that let you know here was a guy who had truly
achieved a rare state of inner with-it-ness. I remember sitting at his feet thinking, "Golly, I could just stay here forever and learn so many wonderful things." He was the very
image of everything a Holy Man from a Mystical Eastern
Spiritual Tradition should be.

A year later I saw Terry's picture in the paper. He was on
the run from the law, wanted in conjunction with a bizarre
murder in West Virginia.

I GAVE UP on Holy Men after that.

Look at the leaders of all the great death and doom religious cults: al-Qaeda, Aum Shinri Kyo, Heaven's Gate, the
Branch Davidians. They've all got the little outfits and that
calm, measured way of speaking. Very comforting, very stilling. No wonder so many people loved those guys enough to

be willing to give up their lives to serve their deranged apoc-
alyptic visions of a New and Better Tomorrow.

I fell for that scam in college, and plenty of people fall
for it every day still. It's a shame how easily people fall for
it. But it's been going on for thousands of years, so it must
be related to some deep desire common throughout
humankind. I don't doubt that the holy rollers of bygone
days were just as seedy and corrupt as the Cadillac-collecting,
womanizing parasites of our own time. The ancestors of
today's spiritual scam-artists go back a long, long way.

So, when I first encountered real Buddhism, I was amazed
to learn that unlike those guys, Buddha never asked his followers to accept what he said just because he said it. He
never told anyone there was any kind of reward waiting for
them after they died if they believed him or any punishment
if they didn't. He just told people what he had learned
through his own experience and invited others to try it out
for themselves because maybe they'd find it useful.

He taught a method by which the individual could experience the truth directly. The word Buddha used for this
method was *dhyana*; in Japan we call it *zazen*, or even just
Zen. *Dhyana* is sometimes translated as meditation, but
it's not what you think it is.

TERRY WAS A PRETTY OBVIOUS SCAM ARTIST, but my own search had
begun such a long time before I met him, I wasn't about to
give up on the whole thing so easily. Starting from about
third grade I'd been obsessed with the problem of Finding
The Truth. As a kid, I came up with (and rejected) all sorts
of bizarre theories: *What if I was just a brain in a jar somewhere being stimulated electrically to believe there was a
real world out there I could interact with?* But that theory
didn't get to the heart of the matter. *Maybe I was a space
alien being raised by human parents*—since my way of
thinking seemed so far removed from that of my peers or

my family. But with no pointy ears, no antennae, and no special powers on account of the yellow sun, I had to relinquish that theory for lack of evidence.

I was a spiritual-minded kid—and I was also impressively bucktoothed. Because of the first trait I tended to be kind of quiet, and because of the second I tended to be ridiculed by the Cool kids at school. I myself was Not Cool and neither were my friends. But they were all real friends. I grew up knowing who I could trust and knowing that most people would do all kinds of rotten, hurtful stuff just to be accepted by society. I didn't want anything to do with that society, and I have never wanted to join any social institution—religions included.

It's only with great reluctance that I call myself "a Buddhist" even today—although I've been involved with Buddhism for the better part of twenty years now. My definition of *Buddhist* has nothing at all to do with the social institutions all over the world that call themselves by that name. Zen Buddhism is direct pointing to the truth. It's cutting through the crap and getting to the ground of things as they really are. It's getting rid of all pretense and seeing what's actually here right now.

Pretty much all the rest of what people call "Buddhism"— the temples, the rituals, the funny outfits, and the ceremonies—isn't the important stuff. It's just decoration. That stuff is useful at times to create a theatrical sort of atmosphere that brings in the crowds, but it's hardly necessary for seeing the reality that the Buddha's teachings point to.

Religions and social institutions aside, I've always felt a need to understand the way things are. It's hard for me to say why. In fact, it's always been far more puzzling to me that more people *don't* feel such a strong need to know. Most of the folks who say they want to understand these things seem to settle for explanations that, as far as I can see, explain things about as well as my childish ideas about being a brain in a jar or a space alien.

A lot of religious explanations remind me of the old joke about the guy who believes the world is flat and rests on the back of a giant turtle. When someone questions him about what's under the turtle, he confidently answers, "Another turtle." When asked what's under *that* turtle he smirks and says, "You can't trip me up with that one! It's turtles all the way down!" Pretty much every religious explanation I've ever run into seems to end up with a variation on "It's turtles all the way down."

I could never accept someone else's version of the truth and I don't think anyone else should. If the meaning of life, the universe, and everything could be put into a few definitive words that everyone on Earth could agree upon now and for all time, someone probably woulda figured them out and written them down. But even if they did, it would still just be *someone else's* truth—not yours. If it seems that within these pages I'm urging you to accept *my* version of the truth, let me apologize now for expressing myself so poorly.

At any rate, because of my experience with Terry and also the whole turtle thing, I'd pretty much ruled out religion as a path to truth. So I thought about science for a while. The idea that there could be a sensible mathematical or scientific solution that we *just haven't quite figured out yet* seemed pretty appealing. But looking into that a little further, it was clear that scientific answers were never really going to do it either, because the best science can ever hope to do is *represent* reality in some way. But that's not enough. Truth has to be bigger than theories, bigger than explanations, bigger than symbols. Truth can't just *explain* everything. It has to *include* everything. It has to *be* everything.

The first time I left behind my own idiosyncratic philosophical theories and got into anything connected with any specific world religion happened while I was living in

Africa. In 1972, when I was eight years old, my dad accepted a transfer from Firestone Tire's Akron headquarters to their new factory in Nairobi, Kenya, where we stayed until 1975. In fourth grade I watched the movie *Jesus Christ Superstar* at a local Nairobi drive-in and then just afterward saw the Nairobi production of *Godspell*. I was eleven then and, man, that Jesus guy was *cool!* I got all my friends together and we made our own version of *Jesus Christ Superstar* called *The Mod Bible*. I, being the writer/director, naturally played Jesus. My best friend Tommy Kashangaki played Saint Peter, and his brother James played Judas Iscariot. My dad shot it all on Super-8—that's Super-8 *film*, kids, this was *way* before home video.

I still cringe when he drags that relic out for people to see, what with me pretending to be nailed to a plywood cross and my sister as Mary Magdalene skipping merrily to the crucifixion. At one point a couple of African women pass by my big death scene in which I dramatically "give up the ghost." God only knows what they must have thought of seeing a little white kid pretending to be nailed to a piece of wood while dying theatrically.

But even then, while faking my own crucifixion, I didn't really believe in religion. It's the same everywhere—we go through the motions but it doesn't mean anything because our beliefs don't get at the root of reality. We take our believing (and our *not* believing too, by the way) for granted, but we rarely ever take a hard look at what belief itself really is.

In college I once passed by a booth being run by some kind of Christian group in the student center. They had a big poster that parodied the poster for the then-current film *Indiana Jones and the Temple of Doom* (what an awful movie *that* was, by the way). In huge yellow letters in the style of the film's logo it said, *REPENT AND TURN TO GOD*. The guy at the booth noticed me looking at the poster and asked me about my beliefs and my relationship to God. Now in those days, I was so punk I rebelled against punk itself by not looking like a punk, and instead sported the dashing look of a stoner. I had long blond hair and dressed exclusively in out-of-fashion bell-bottoms and ratty black T-shirts. The dude in the booth was clean-cut with neatly trimmed hair and a nice conservative suit with the mandatory blue tie. I must have looked like a real prize to him. I'm sure he thought that if he could convert such an obvious heathen as me, he'd definitely get a gold star from God.

But I honestly wanted to know about this whole matter of belief so I asked the guy to explain it to me. The gist of his explanation went something like this: "If a person believed Jesus actually literally did all the miraculous things he's supposed to have done, that person would be scared of Jesus' power and would therefore be converted to Christianity. Furthermore, lots of people who actually witnessed Jesus' miracles with their own eyes chose to die rather than deny what they'd seen. Therefore the Bible is literally true, and therefore we should all be scared. So, *REPENT AND TURN TO GOD.*"

Like I said, religions never did a lot for me.

Religious people always seemed like they wanted to squeeze my imagination into a little box—and I didn't even get to decorate the box! My head always hurt listening to these guys. Why was it so important to believe in certain things particularly? Why was it so essential to believe that a long time ago in some part of the world I've never been to, someone walked barefoot across a pond without getting wet? What does that have to do with my life right here and right now?

UNLIKE RELIGIONS, Zen doesn't have a set system of beliefs for you to adopt. One thing that's always impressed me about

Buddhists is that they don't give a damn about the fact that it's widely known that many of the words attributed to Buddha were written hundreds of years after his death. "Who cares?" the devout Buddhists say. Because it doesn't matter one way or the other. The only thing Buddhists believe in is the reality of the world in which we are all living right now. Buddhism is based on your real life as it is, not on whether or not you believe there's an old guy with a beard above the clouds who will smite you or hand you a harp.

Religion doesn't have a monopoly on truth. In fact, if you're anything like me religion is one of the last places you'll look for truth.

For me, music seemed a much more likely candidate.

INNER ANARCHY

Punk rock is just an excuse
for troublemakers who want to
mess up the system.
FRANK "PONCH" PONCHARELLO
(PLAYED BY ERIK ESTRADA) ON CHIPS

WHEN I WAS FOURTEEN, I asked my parents for a set of drums. Instead, they got me an orange Stella acoustic guitar with a lame little butterfly on the pick-guard—and *bang* I was on my way to discovering a new source of truth, something far more meaningful, far more real than any religion in the world, namely: *rock and roll.*

From that time on, rock and roll was my life. But everything playing on the radio in those days—the mid-to-late '70s—was unbelievably lame. I don't mean that there was *a lot* of worthless garbage on radio. I mean that *every single piece of music you heard on any rock radio station* in those days was absolute doggie-do. The most popular bands of the day, corporate rockers like Styx, REO Speedwagon, and Journey, played music that was so bland, so joyless, so unrelentingly, wretchedly *awful* it was hard to imagine it hadn't been scientifically designed to induce vomiting— you know, like the stuff the doctors give you to make you puke up the quart Liquid-Plumr® you swallowed when your were four. On a good day, maybe it was elevator music with a backbeat. These days you'd be hard pressed to find anyone who'll admit they liked that stuff. Yet it sold by the truck-load back then. Imagine.

The only good music to be found on the radio then was on the oldies stations. I began to believe that all the good rock music that could ever be made had been made by the time I got to kindergarten. But in the fall of 1978, just after I'd started eighth grade I saw DEVO on *Saturday Night Live* and lo, I knew the gods of rock and roll were not yet dead.

EXCEPT FOR THOSE THREE YEARS in Africa, I grew up in a town called Wadsworth, Ohio, a suburb of Akron about an hour's drive south of Cleveland. As you might imagine, cultural trends are, shall we say, *slow* to hit backwaters like Wadsworth. We didn't even have cable TV. The only place you could get records was at Ben Franklin's Five & Ten which carried a selection of about nine different rock titles, maybe.

It wasn't until I saw DEVO on TV that I had any inkling any good rock still existed, although I'd heard about DEVO before then. The Akron papers had been full of stories of the so-called Akron new wave rock scene. But being underage and unable to drive into the "big city," I had no means by which to experience it for myself. The fashions certainly looked interesting—but I'd never heard the music. DEVO turned my little head around and gave me a reason to live.

And, wonder of wonders, Ben Franklin's actually had a copy of their first LP! So I saved up my allowance and bought it—then played it until the grooves wore down. After I got my driver's license I spent all my time and whatever cash I could scrounge searching for new wave and punk records and magazines. My friend Mike Duffy (one of about four other people in Wadsworth who were into this stuff) and I got together our own new wave band called Mmaxx. Mmaxx played a total of four gigs, consisting of two nerdy dances held by the speech and debate teams at Wadsworth High, a party at my friend Cindy Choi's house, and one bonus gig. I remember Cindy's dad rockin' out to our out-of-tune covers of The Ramones and Gary Numan. He liked us so much he invited us to play at a party he was holding the following weekend for a bunch of his friends from work. That second party was an unqualified disaster— those guys did not take well to their cocktails being spoiled by our brand of noise.

But Mmaxx got one big break. I took our demo tape to the manager of The Bank, the legendary venue in Akron where all the cool new-wave groups had played. The Bank had once been a real bank: there was a giant vault inside as well as the vestiges of teller's windows and the luxurious lobby that once lured major investors to put their money into what had been, some fifty years earlier, one of America's fastest-growing cities. To my astonishment we got the gig. But The Bank, as it turned out, was only months away from closing its doors forever. The management had changed several times and the guy who was running the place now would take whoever he could get. Bands had fought like mad to get shows there only a year earlier, and groups who'd played The Bank had gone on to sign lucrative deals with big record labels. Not many people remember it anymore but in the late '70s Akron, Ohio, was considered a real hotbed of new trends in music—much like Seattle after Nirvana got big. Talent scouts from New York and Los Angeles had hung out at The Bank looking for the Next Big Thing. But that was last year. This year no one wanted to go near the place.

Alas, our big gig at The Bank was not to be. Mike and I were old men of seventeen and had liberal parents who believed our promises that, although The Bank was a bar, we wouldn't be drinking. And it was true. Neither of us had any interest in alcohol at that point. We just wanted to rock. Our drummer, Mark, on the other hand was just a wee babe of fifteen. His parents put their foot down. Their son would *not* be playing drums in a bar at such a tender young age—and that was effectively the end of Mmaxx. We tried to get another drummer, but the only guy in Wadsworth who was even willing to consider the job wanted us to play a few "real rock" numbers of the sad ilk mentioned above. Our punked-up versions of Led Zeppelin's *Rock and Roll* and Ted Nugent's *Cat Scratch Fever* didn't cut it with him. So, vaguely reminiscent of my performance on the fake crucifix, our band gave up the ghost.

SOMETIME late in my senior year of high school, I saw an ad in *Scene*, Cleveland's free music paper, saying that the band Zero Defex was auditioning bass players. I'd seen Zero Defex twice at The Bank, each time with a different bass player. They were the hardest, fastest, and loudest of the Akron hardcore punk scene. Hardcore punk took the original philosophy of punk ten steps further: the fast tempos were twice as fast, the simple melodies transformed into shouting, the short haircuts gave way to shaved heads, and energetic pogo-dancing became people running around crashing into each other like dodge-'em cars

And Zero Defex took the hardcore punk further than anyone else on the scene was willing to go. The other bands I'd seen play with them still had identifiable songs, some of which lasted vast durations of two minutes or more. Every Zero Defex song was about fifteen to thirty seconds long and none of them could be distinguished from the others in any meaningful way. A whole Zero Defex set was over and done in the time it took other bands just to tune up. *My God,* I thought the first time I'd seen them play, *This is it. This is the Real Deal.* The hardest thing I'd heard up till then was the Ramones album *End of the Century.* Seeing Zero Defex was like a religious revelation for me.

Needless to say, I answered the ad (in fact I discovered later I was the only one who answered it) and was directed to band's rehearsal space, a dilapidated old house in a seedy part of Akron called North Hill. Five or six punk rockers shared the rent at the place, though you could always count on there being twice that number just hanging out on any given day. Two of the residents had kids and so the place had been nicknamed The Mommy Dearest Daycare Center. The place was the foulest, dirtiest, stinkiest house I'd ever set foot in. There was trash all over the floor: cigarette butts, empty beer cans, junk food packages, you name it. There were piles of records in various states of disarray all over the place and a cruddy old record player that never stopped grinding tinny-sounding low-budget punk records out of even tinnier-sounding speakers. On one ripped-up old couch I saw two bald people making out. It took me a minute to work out that one of them was a girl.

I was led down to the basement and handed a sticker-encrusted Fender Musicmaster bass plugged into a nameless amp with a blown speaker. It didn't even sound like a musical instrument, kinda more like a sumo wrestler with a case of squelchy farts. I played a few scales to warm up. Hearing me do this, the skinhead singer, whose real name was James Friend but who called himself Jimi Imij, said in a disgusted tone, "Oh, a *real* musician."

The guitar player, Tommy Strange (aka Tom Seiler), another skinhead,* showed me some of their songs, which I was surprised to learn actually had set chord changes, contrary to their appearance of total randomness—though

* Though their heads were shaved and they often called themselves "skinheads" neither Jimi, Tommy, nor any of the other "skins" in the early '80s Akron scene were the kind of neo-Nazi, right-wing racist skinheads that existed in some other areas. In fact they were almost annoyingly left-wing and decidedly anti-racist.

Tommy wasn't uncool enough to admit he actually knew the names of any of the chords he was playing. He'd just show me the riffs at full breakneck speed and I was expected to work them out. When I asked him to slow down so I could at least watch what he was doing he shot me a withering glance of disdain. But their stuff was all dirt simple, even easier than the Ramones covers I'd been playing before that. I got the whole set down in an afternoon and I was in.

I gradually learned that in spite of their pose, the hardcores hadn't just sprung up from the earth fully formed. I'd assumed that drummer Mickey Nelson was the only member who used his real name until I learned he had played bass in a surf group called The Nelsons, one of the last of the first wave of Akron new wave bands and a fairly popular draw a year or so earlier. Like The Ramones, The Nelsons all used the same last name on stage. Mickey's real last name was Hurray—which sounded more like a made-up name to me than Nelson. Tommy had been in The Bursting Brains, probably northeast Ohio's first hardcore band. Jimi Imij had played in The V-Nervz, an early punk (though not hardcore) outfit, but was more well known for being one of the people who hung out with German avant-garde musician Klaus Nomi when he'd briefly relocated to Akron to pick up on the scene there in the late '70s. (Klaus was back in West Germany at that point, though a bit later he was one of the first celebrities to die of AIDS—which gave Jimi quite a scare.)

I ended up with a punk name too, by the way. I was Brad No Sweat, since I was the only one who didn't work up a sweat on stage. I guess all punk names can't be cool. These days, though, I'm just as unlikely to go by No Sweat as by my other fake name, Odo, which I received when I was ordained as a Buddhist priest. My experience with Terry sorta soured me on the whole "spiritual name" thing, so everyone pretty much calls me "Brad" (or in the case of my Japanese friends, *Buraddo-san*).

The punk scene continued to grow in Akron for about two years. Aside from Zero Defex, notable bands included Starvation Army, The Urban Mutants, and The Agitated. Cleveland bands like The Offbeats, The Guns, and The Dark came down to Akron for gigs too. Zero Defex even got as far afield as exotic Detroit and Toledo. We made the trips in a rusted-out old Dodge van dense-packed with as many guitars, amps, drums, and punk rockers as physically possible. I remember me and Fraser Suicyde, the singer of Starvation Army, getting paranoid about the way the exhaust was flowing into the cab of the van and finding a large rust hole on the side, through which we took turns trying to suck in some comparatively cleaner air. On one of these trips the driver, Andy, brought along a used love doll he'd found in a Dumpster™—every time a car got close to us, Fraser and I crouched down out of view, lifted the love doll up to the back window and made her wave. Boy did we know how to have a good time!

THINGS STARTED TO GO BAD for Zero Defex about a year later when we got a gig in Dover, Ohio, even more of a backwoods town than Wadsworth—something I'd have scarcely thought possible. While Wadsworth was a fairly conservative burg populated by businessmen who worked in Akron and their families, the proverbial "nice place to raise your kids," Dover was a true *Deliverance*-style rural hell-hole full of rednecks in dirty flannel shirts who drove mudencrusted pickup trucks. Yet somehow a kind of new wave scene had emerged at a bar down there with the unlikely name of The Spanish Ballroom. A band called Johnny Clampett and the Walkers, who played new wave versions of '50s and '60s tunes, had established themselves there and used to bring other slightly more adventurous bands from

Akron and Kent down to support them. Someone had convinced the bar's owners that hardcore punk might be worth a try, so Zero Defex and Starvation Army, Akron's two most popular hardcore bands (meaning we could maybe draw crowds of twenty people on a good night), got booked down there on an off night.

From the moment when we first set foot in that joint, we knew this was *not* a punk rock crowd. There were about fifteen people inside, most of them slumped listlessly over the long red bar. A dozen or so tables stood empty in the middle of the room. There wasn't a skinhead or even a Sid Vicious–style razor-cut in sight. No leather jackets, no striped shirts, no skinny ties. These were hardcore people all right—hardcore bikers, truck drivers, and factory workers complete with long hair, scraggly beards, and beer-guts. There were a couple of women with bleached blonde hair done up in giant Farrah Fawcett–style do's. The bar owner assured us that these were just "the regulars" and they'd clear out in an hour or so and the new wavers would show up.

Cautiously we set up our equipment on what passed for a stage. It wasn't even a raised platform, just a slightly less cluttered space on the floor between some speaker cabinets that also served as the PA system. We didn't want to sound-check in front of these guys since they were already starting to froth at the mouth as they eyeballed our assorted mohawks, skinheads, and metal-studded jackets. A few hours passed but the regulars never left. In fact several more of them arrived. Not a single new waver or punk showed up. By 10:30 the bar owner was telling us we'd better get started.

I was the one who looked most like these people, having never cut my shoulder length hair into a more "punky" style or gone in for the punk get-up of a black leather jacket and army boots. So The Eric Nipplehead Project (ENP), a side band I'd put together with the guitarist and drummer from Starvation Army to play instrumental surf tunes, was elected to go on first. We played eight numbers, spanning about fifteen minutes, and it seemed to go fairly well. We had the *Batman* TV show theme song and Gary Glitter's *Rock and Roll Part 2* in our set—which these *Deliverance* guys could sort of relate to. We got heckled a bit, but it was nothing we couldn't shrug off. I got the feeling some of them almost liked us.

But that was it. ENP was all the normality we collectively had to offer. Next up was Zero Defex. I moved over from guitar, which I played with ENP, to bass, and as soon as skinheads Tommy Strange and Jimi Imij took the floor, it was clear there was going to be trouble. We got successfully through our first song, *Drop the A-Bomb on Me*—but only because, at eighteen seconds, it was too short for any of the alcohol-addled regulars to react to before it was over. When we launched into *Die Before More of This*, a guy with a red ZZ-Top beard whipped a wicked-looking hunting knife out of his jeans jacket and sliced Jimi Imij's mic cord in half.

We didn't have time to appreciate the irony that the PA system belonged to the bar and not to us before the brawl broke out. Chairs and beer bottles flew and crashed into walls and tables. I ducked into the ladies' room and hid in a locked stall, scared for my life. Someone ran outside and flagged down a cop and things quieted down. We even got a police escort out of town—probably the only time in the history of hardcore that the cops protected the punks. Mickey, our drummer, went home with a fractured leg, though other injuries were mild. Apparently the bar was known for this kind of behavior. I found out later that my friend Johnny Phlegm's Greenburst Burns bass had been trashed by one of these same rednecks at the same bar only months before under similar circumstances. Why Zero Defex ever accepted a gig there after that had happened is still a mystery to me. We evidently didn't do our research.

I didn't quit the band after that, but that incident took a lot of the drive to continue the movement out of me. Sure I wanted to shake up the complacent contemporary music scene—but I didn't want to get killed doing it. Zero Defex broke up in the Summer of 1984. By that time punk had already started to turn turgid and conservative. It no longer showed the spirit it had even two years earlier. At first, punks had dressed the way they did to show their individuality. But by 1984 the leather jackets, tight jeans, badges, and short haircuts had turned into a uniform. When I used to show up with long hair and tie-dyed shirts, guys in mohawks would yell at me to cut my hair—just like the rednecks in pickup trucks did when I walked around like that outside. What was the difference? None that I could see.

The punks weren't real nonconformists—they just had a different standard they thought people should conform to.

IN ITS EARLY DAYS, punk had a lot in common with Zen. It wasn't just the fetish for shaved heads and black clothes, either. The attitude of not conforming blindly to society is an important aspect of Buddhist teaching. One thing that really endeared me to my current Zen teacher, a guy named Gudo Nishijima, was when I heard him talking about the new styles of dress that were becoming popular in Japan. The bizarre, bright hair dyes, strange-looking makeup, and outlandish clothes teenagers were getting into reminded me of the way my friends had looked fifteen years earlier. These weren't just imitations of the older punk look (though there was a lot of that too), but a completely new Japanese style. I expected Nishijima, a Buddhist monk in his late seventies, to be critical of them. But he wasn't. Instead he said these trends were representative of a more realistic outlook he believed was emerging in all of humanity. "They dress the way they want to," he said, "not because society tells them how to dress. And that is very important."

Question authority. Question society. Question reality.

But you've got to take it all the way: Question punk authority. Question punk society. Question your own rules and question your own values. Question Zen society. Question Zen authority. Question other people's views on reality and question your own.

No matter what authority you submit to—your teacher, your government, even Jesus H. Christ or Gautama Buddha himself—that authority is wrong. It's wrong because the very *concept* of authority is already a mistake. Deferring to authority is nothing more than a cowardly shirking of personal responsibility. The more power you grant an authority figure the worse you can behave in his name. That's why people who take God as their ultimate authority are always capable of the worst humanity has to offer. Zen does not accept anything even resembling that kind of God.

If you aim to tear down authority, doing so honestly means doing so completely. Really tearing down authority means more than just opposing the big government and big business. You need to tear out the very *roots* of authority. This can never be done through violence of any kind—not ever—because the ultimate authority is your own belief in the very concept of authority. Revolt against *that* first. You need the courage to take responsibility for your own life and your own actions.

People have taken exception to my equating a noble tradition like Zen Buddhism with a scrappy upstart thing like punk rock. Zen Buddhism is ancient and venerable. Punk is trash. But punk is a cultural movement that was made possible only because of the increased understanding of reality that emerged in the twentieth century, the so-called postmodern worldview. The punks understood that all social institutions and socially approved codes of dress and behavior were a sham. This is one of the first steps to true understanding. It's unfortunate that not many punks actually followed through to what punk really implied: that *all* of our values need to be questioned. It's typical for a minority social movement to throw away the accepted rules of society. But they almost always end up just substituting another set of rules for the ones they've challenged.

In spite of their talk about anarchy and "no rules" the punks quickly developed a very rigid set of rules of their own. Anarchy was just a symbol, a cool-looking letter "A" inside a circle. Big deal. Real anarchy has to come from deep within. Real anarchy isn't immoral or amoral; it's *intensely* moral. A pseudo-anarchist spraypaints a letter "A" in a circle on the side of a government building "to make a point." A *true* anarchist understands that action in the present moment is what really matters and lives his life accordingly. Painting letters on buildings doesn't accomplish anything except giving the poor grunts who do the building maintenance some extra work. No one's going to see that letter "A" and decide to learn more about the philosophy of anarchy.

Questioning society's values is a great and important thing to do. But that's easy compared to questioning your own values. Questioning your own values means really questioning yourself, really looking at who and what you believe and who you are.

Who are you?

That's where Buddhism comes into the picture. Stay tuned.

ZEN &the ART OF MAKING MONSTER MOVIES

...then you have your fear, which could be reality, and you have Godzilla, which is *reality.*
RAYMOND BURR in GODZILLA: KING OF THE MONSTERS

FOLLOWING THE BREAK-UP of Zero Defex in 1984, I discovered the music of Syd Barrett, ex-leader of Pink Floyd, whose solo albums were full of weird dreamlike imagery set to even weirder tunes. It was as if his music were pop hits that had been written on Silly Putty® then stretched and compressed all out of proportion. Inspired by Syd Barrett, I started making lots of demos of my own neo-psychedelic songs. The Meat Puppets, with whom Zero Defex had played in 1983, had moved from hardcore punk to weird '60s-influenced guitar freakouts, thereby proving there was some kind of market for psychedelia in the '80s. But the clear white light hit me when I went to see a band called Plan 9 at a bar in Kent called JB's Down. It was a nine-piece group with an astounding number of guitarists (four!). The number of people in the band was larger than the number of people in the audience that night. But it was the sound that got me. Plan 9 played garage rock in the style of a thousand snotty teenage bands from the '60s. Think *I'm Not Your Stepping Stone* by The Monkees. Years later Oasis would rip off this sound, mix it with some Beatles influences, and pretend it was all brand new. When I saw Plan 9, that was it for me. I had—once again—found The Way.

IT WAS EASY TO TALK to the band afterward. I bought their album and discovered it was on a label called Midnight Records out of New York. They told me Midnight was looking for new artists, so I sent the label some of my crude demos. Several months later, I heard from JD Martignon, the owner of Midnight Records. He'd liked the demos and wanted to put something out. By "something" I assumed he meant a cut on a compilation or maybe a single. When I called him back he said, in a heavy French accent, "I want you to—'ow you say?—make ze album." *Gulp.*

It was to be a "P&D" deal, he said, meaning Midnight would press and distribute the album but I had to supply the master tapes, recorded at my own expense. I had six hundred bucks in the bank, and the studio where Zero Defex had once recorded charged twenty dollars an hour. I did the math on exactly how long it would take to exhaust my life's savings and worked out how I could record the ten tracks needed to make up a standard LP on that kind of budget. This meant knowing all the arrangements up-front and going in and recording everything in a single take. Mixdowns? *I don't need no steenking mix-downs!* I'd done all my demos alone, crudely overdubbing the instruments by playing along to cassettes of myself while simultaneously using a second cassette machine to record the results. If I involved anyone else, I risked messing up my carefully laid plans, so I decided to go it alone. The total budget for the first album by Dimentia 13, the name I'd chosen when JD told me records by solo artists never sold, came in at $575. It came out in 1986 to great reviews in the underground magazines and sold respectably.

AT THE TIME, I was still a student at Kent State University, searching for some kind of academic direction. I'd dropped my communications major and switched to art; but after practically flunking out of art I'd started taking classes more or less at random hoping something would click. I was taking a lot of philosophy and I signed up for a class called Zen Buddhism. The prof was a scrawny, nerdy-looking white guy named Tim McCarthy, miles removed from anyone's image of a Zen master. He wasn't old, he wasn't Japanese, he didn't have a shaved head, he didn't wear black robes. And he didn't talk in that appalling tone of voice so many representatives of "mystical" religions like my old Krishna buddy Terry like to adopt. He was funny, he was loud, he was real—and he was simply himself. He peppered his speech with references to comic books and weird noises that sounded like duck calls. At the same time, it was evident to me that he was a very serious person. He was completely upfront about who he was.

He was a guy, just like me. He claimed no exalted titles and didn't try to bowl anyone over with clever phrases or enlightened-sounding talk. He made no promises he had or could deliver enlightenment, or anything else for that matter. He was just Tim. If what he said sounded interesting to you, he'd tell you some more. If you weren't interested, it was no skin off his ass—and that attitude made me very interested indeed. I'd never come across a representative of any religion who wasn't trying to convince me of something, who wasn't trying to sell me on his faith, who, in fact, didn't give two shits whether I believed in or even listened to what he had to say.

In my first class with Tim, he gave a lecture about the Heart Sutra that so profoundly rocked my mental world that I've devoted a chapter to it later on in this book. He also introduced the class to the practice of zazen, which was what the Zen school calls the kind of meditation they do.

Meditation was definitely not *de rigueur* for Kent State University. In spite of its reputation as a "radical school" following the events of May 4, 1970, KSU was about as lame and conservative as any state-run university anywhere in America. The whole class was pretty taken aback when Tim whipped out a couple dozen black cushions from a duffel bag, had us sit cross-legged on them, and told us just to be still and stare straight ahead at the walls. Blinking was fine and scratching or shifting positions was okay as long as we didn't do too much of it. We weren't given any mantras to think about, nothing to visualize, no instructions on counting our breath—*nada*. There was no sitar music playing in the background (though he did light up a stick of incense). He told us just to stay that way for the next twenty minutes.

Twenty minutes?! I thought, along with everyone else in the class. *Sitting still?! Not doing anything?!* Half the kids in that class nearly died of shock at the very thought.

Me, though, I was into it. I'd been trying to meditate on and off ever since I'd read some descriptions of the practice in one of the Hare Krishna magazines. But the Hare Krishnas, I later learned, don't go for the whole idea of silent meditation. To them, chanting *"Hare Krishna"* is the only way to achieve what they call *transcendental consciousness*. The descriptions of silent meditation practices in their magazines and books are full of stuff about guys who cut the tendons on the bottoms of their tongues so they can stick them up their noses and similar gross-out stories (though frankly the spiritual benefit of such behavior is not immediately apparent to me). For all I knew at the time, they were the voice of authority on the subject. And I wasn't about to slice up my tongue.

So I eventually gave up pursuing meditation. But from Tim I was getting instruction from someone who actually knew how to do it and actually did it himself. I figured I'd be seeing visions of four-armed Krishnas and Vishnus descending from the heavens in no time flat. Or maybe I'd fade into The Void just like in The Beatles' song "Tomorrow Never Knows." I might even reach nirvana (I think I'd read about that once in a *Mad* magazine cartoon). But the clock just ticked away, my legs started aching, and stupid thoughts kept drifting into my head. Maybe I wasn't doing it right, I figured. Maybe I was missing something crucial. Maybe what I was doing on my cushion with my stupid mind as I was staring dumbly at the wall wasn't quite it.

Now I can look back after twenty years of practice and say: *Nope—that was it.* Boring, boring, boring. Just sitting there. But even then, from that first day, there was something about zazen that just felt somehow *right*.

It was a practice that demanded nothing at all—and everything. There were no specific demands or instructions on what I was actually supposed to *do* as I sat there, but that very fact demanded that I had to make the practice valuable *for myself.* Now, I've always been a guy who had to be doing something at all times. I don't like vegging out the way lots of people do. I'd gotten into art and music mainly because I felt I had to *produce something* in order to justify any activity I found enjoyable. I don't like to waste time. Ever. Zazen gave me a way do nothing while still doing something that seemed somehow constructive.

Another thing I appreciated about Zen Buddhism was that it was resolutely anti-sexist. The other religions I'd encountered, including the Hare Krishnas as representatives of "Eastern spirituality," were very much boys' clubs. Since high school most of my closest friends had been female. My friend Emily once called me a "womanly man." I'm still not sure how to take that. And with my long hair and rather slender physique (I prefer that description to "wimpy"), by college I'd had more experience than most guys of being propositioned by hard-up horny-toads in

Trans Ams. Buddha was emphatic that women were just as capable as men of reaching enlightenment.

I made the practice of zazen part of my daily routine from that day on. But I certainly wasn't ready to commit to the life of a Zen monk, whatever I imagined that might be, because, after all, I was a rising star in the indie music scene! In 1987 I made another record, and the next year I actually put together a real band and played live a few times. Our third album, *Disturb the Air*, was produced by Glenn Rehse of the band Plasticland. That one sounded like a real record. The vocals were mostly on-key, and I even did multiple takes of certain tracks to try to get things right— because by this time Midnight Records was paying the studio bills. Glenn played Mellotron, the keyboard made famous by The Beatles and The Moody Blues for its ability to imitate a full orchestra (albeit a spooky, slightly out-of-tune full orchestra) and mixed the results with slabs of cavernous reverb making our little garage band sound positively *huge*. Our record sales, unfortunately, failed to live up to the hugeness of our sound.

AS I WAS DOING all that zazen and was struggling to make Dimentia 13 happen, another strange idea was brewing in my brain. Ever since I was a little kid, there was something compelling for me about Japanese monster movies. I couldn't tell you for certain what it was. But in the 1970s movies like *Godzilla: King of the Monsters*, *Gammera the Invincible*, *War of the Gargantuas*, and *Frankenstein Conquers the World* (in which a fifty-foot-tall Frankenstein monster terrorizes Tokyo then dukes it out with a big-ass dinosaur) were staples of UHF television. In Cleveland most of these films were hosted by The Ghoul, Channel 61's hepcat horror host with a fake goatee and groovy green wig who came on during the commercial segments of his Saturday late-night show to talk trash about the movies and blow up model kits with M80 firecrackers. I was mesmerized by every one of those stupid rubber dino-fests.

But even better than Godzilla & Co. was a Japanese science fiction TV series called *Ultraman*, which came on every Monday, Wednesday, and Friday at 4:30 in the afternoon on channel 43. (Tuesday and Thursday they showed another Japanese sci-fi program called *Johnny Sokko and His Flying Robot.**) Unlike most kids' shows, *Ultraman* was not a cartoon. It was a live-action show with special effects like the original *Star Trek*. The hero was a silver-and-red guy with big yellow bug-eyes on a sinister, immobile, and totally alien metallic face that predated the Greys from the *X-Files* by thirty years. But what really set Ultraman apart from American superheros was that he was 150 feet tall. And he didn't battle boring bank robbers and criminal masterminds either. Not our Ultraman. No way. He personally slugged it out with gigantic Godzilla-style monsters.

Why *Ultraman* affected me so deeply I can't really say. But I do know that I got my very first taste of Buddhism from an episode of the show. It was episode 35, in fact, known in Japan as *"Kaiju Hakaba"*—"The Graveyard of Monsters." The main cast of the *Ultraman* TV show was the Science Patrol, a five-person super-scientific fighting force who seemed to be the only people able to do anything when Tokyo was getting trampled by a rampant iguana with a glandular condition. In this episode, the Science Patrol decides they feel pretty bad about having slaughtered so many gigantic creatures whose only crime was that they were too big to walk down Tokyo's boulevards without wrecking everything (not unlike most American tourists actually). So the Science Patrol holds a traditional Japanese Buddhist funeral service for all the monsters they'd killed. A group of monks pound a traditional wooden drum shaped like a fish, burn incense, and chant

---

*Not nearly as good.

in front of photos of the dead beasts adorned with the traditional black ribbons. It was cool.

I loved Japanese monster movies and I knew deep in my
heart that Japan was where I wanted to be. I fantasized
about how these movies were made. I used to imagine a
room full of rubber monster costumes hanging from hooks
on the ceiling. I'd pray that someday magic would happen
and I'd come home to find that room when I opened the
door to the attic above our garage. (The room I fantasized
about, by the way, was exactly like the Monster Warehouse
at Tsuburaya Productions, a place I never even suspected
really existed back then. It's even in an attic that looks a
whole lot like the one at the house I lived in then—but I'm
getting ahead of the story here.)

In those days I devoured everything I could get my hot
little hands on about Japan and its monsters. Mind you, in
Wadsworth, Ohio, in the '70s, that wasn't much. I had a
few copies of *Famous Monsters of Filmland* and *Monster
Times* magazines with Godzilla in them. As a teenager I
even made my own Japanese-style (i.e., really bad and low-
budget) monster movies. I borrowed my dad's old Super-8
camera and drafted my friends into service as actors and
special-effects assistants. Each cartridge held about ten
minutes' worth of silent film, so we'd go out and spend an
afternoon making a ten-minute monster movie. It never
occurred to us that maybe real moviemakers actually wrote
scripts before shooting their movies; we'd just make it up
as we went along.

When the film was about three-quarters used up and
nothing significant had happened, we'd try to think of a cli-
max. Then, when the film was almost completely gone,
we'd have to come up with an ending. Whenever we came
to a special effects sequence, the "actors" would take five
while I and the "special effects crew"—which invariably
included some, if not all, of the "actors"—went over and

animated my collection of Aurora dinosaur models. Editing? *We don't need no steenking editing!* Thus came into being such cinematic masterpieces as *Buck Laserbreath and Rocky Cosmic Disorders on the Planet of Dinosaurs* and *Voyage to the Outer Space Trek. Mad* magazine would have been proud.

When I finally got out of Wadsworth and into Kent State University I took Japanese to fulfill my language requirement. I got C-minuses, but only because the teacher was too nice to fail me. I thought I'd never realize my dream of actually setting foot in the Promised Land.

Then around 1990, my sister heard about a thing called the Japan Exchange and Teaching (JET) program run by the Japanese government's ministry of education. They were actually paying young Americans good money to come to Japan and teach Japanese kids real live English.

By this time Dimentia 13 had released its fifth album, *Flat Earth Society,* to a thunderous roar of critical and public indifference. I was sharing a place nicknamed The Clubhouse in Akron's seedy North Hill district with Steve, the current drummer for Dimentia 13, and Logan, lead singer of the Zen Luv Assassins (who had no Zen influences at all, mind you, save for Logan's penchant for black clothes), and Logan's girlfriend Laura. Sitting on the john in our small bathroom, you could view the kitchen table through a hole in the floor. The wall of the shower was held together by duct tape and an inch-thick layer of mold. You couldn't get through the living room without tripping over dead guitars and cannibalized amplifiers. And if you survived that obstacle course, you'd be felled by the odor of a litterbox that hadn't been properly cleaned in months.

There were many times when raising the sixty-five bucks for rent was a major problem for me. I worked lousy temp jobs and survived on packages of Kraft® Macaroni & Cheese. Not that any of this was new to me; this was a lifestyle I had enjoyed, with minor variations here and there, for the better part of a decade. The Golden Prosperity of the Reagan Years *my ass!* I wanted out.

THE JET PROGRAM only accepts applications during certain months, so it took me nearly a year to get it together to get my application in. By then my circumstances had improved slightly. The band wasn't doing much better but I had a steadier day job as an instructor for mentally handicapped adults, "consumers" as we euphemistically called them.

I moved out of that rathole in Akron and into a house Tim McCarthy, the Zen teacher I'd met at KSU, had dubbed the Kent Zendo (*zendo* means "place you practice Zen"). That place was run down too, but the people there actually made some effort to keep it reasonably clean and keep everything in good working order. The Kent Zendo motto was: "We're the smallest." Say what you will, at least we weren't guilty of false advertising.

The living room was cleared out for holding zazen practice and a small altar stood at one end of the room, just to the left of the door to the toilet. Once, I made the mistake of leaving my camera unattended and much later when I developed the film, I found a shot of Tim pointing his willy at the little statue of the Buddha on the altar.

At the time I lived there, it was tough for Tim to get a lot of people interested in Buddhism. Only one of the other six people in the house was into it at all. The rest were Kent State University students who were not into subtle Eastern teachings so much as cheap rent. The weekly sittings would be attended by between five and ten people, mostly college students who showed up once or twice then promptly gave up when they didn't find enlightenment right away.

As for me, I'd go through phases of being really hot on the practice and sitting at least two forty-minute periods every day, then getting frustrated and doing a token five or ten minutes half-assedly before bed. I rarely went more than a day or two without doing it at all, though. Whenever I stopped, I felt it: my brain just wasn't right.

Even with my new job, I was still destitute. Midnight Records wasn't selling enough Dimentia 13 albums to make me any extra cash and the major labels I kept sending my stuff to never bothered to even write back with rejections. I became increasingly convinced that all my problems would be solved *if only* I could earn a little bit of money and fulfill my dream of living in the land of Ultraman. I never actually believed money could buy me happiness. But not having money certainly seemed to be hooking me up with a lifetime supply of pains in the ass.

At any rate, before too long I got a letter from the JET program saying the Japanese government was willing to pay me more than *three times* what I'd been earning up 'til then—plus half my rent in Japan!—to go to their wonderful monster-filled country and teach their lovely children to talk just like me. *Sweet!*

SMALL & STUPID DREAMS

Suppose you are thinking of a plate
of shrimp. Suddenly somebody'll say, like,
"plate" or "shrimp" or "plate of shrimp."
No explanation. No point in looking
for one one, either. It's all part
of the cosmic unconsciousness.

MILLER (PLAYED BY TRACEY WALTER)
FROM THE MOVIE REPO MAN

WORKED HARD to improve my pathetic Japanese skills during my first year in Japan. At the end of year one I re-upped for a second year with JET. I would spend another year teaching in Japan—or rather, talking in English in front of groups of sleeping teenagers, which the Japanese ministry of education was kind enough to regard as "teaching." It was arguably the dumbest job in the world, but I still liked it.

In a bookstore, I saw a book called *Tsuburaya Noboru Urutoraman Wo Kataru*—"Noboru Tsuburaya Talks about Ultraman"—by the president and CEO of Tsuburaya Productions, the company that made *Ultraman*, and the son of the late Eiji Tsuburaya who'd created the original Godzilla. Obviously, despite the fact that the book had absolutely no pictures of gigantic half-crab/half-alligator beasts walloping Tokyo Tower or huge spacemen shooting laserbeams from their fingertips, I had to buy it. In fact, it had no pictures at all save for the one of Noboru himself on the back flap (it turns out he looks like a Japanese man, by the way), and yet I was determined to read this thing, pictures or no.

And I actually did read about a third of it. And of that third I probably understood about an eighth. Still, one thing was very clear: Noboru Tsuburaya had dreams of Ultraman one day cracking the U.S. market and getting as big in America as he was in Japan. And believe you me, Ultraman is *very* big in Japan. His expressionless face adorns everything from key chains to golf-club covers to condoms (the packages, not the actual condoms—*that* would be a little weird). With virtually no sales outside of Asia, Ultraman still earned enough licensing revenue in the 1980s to make him the third top-selling licensed character in the world right behind Mickey Mouse™ and Charlie Brown.™ And who on Earth would be better to sell Ultraman to the Americans than me? Nobody, dammit. Obviously.

So I decided I'd write Noboru Tsuburaya a letter and tell him so. My girlfriend Yuka (who is now my wife) kindly fixed all the grammatical mistakes and showed me how to type it out on the Japanese word processor at my school. Off the letter went. I waited and waited (and waited) and no reply came.

So I decided to write again.

Why not? Stamps were cheap and my job was pretty boring. This time I made it more clear that I was just exactly the kind of guy he needed to help realize his dreams of "making Ultraman fly over America." From the book, I could tell the guy was a bit of an egomaniac—so I laid the praise on with a trowel. I didn't lie though; I really was genuinely impressed by him, and especially by his father, and their work had deeply touched me and utterly transformed my life giving me meaning where before there was none. Okay, maybe I exaggerated that last bit a little.

A while later I came home one afternoon after a day of shouting over gossiping kids to find my answering machine blinking. I pressed the button figuring it'd be one of the members of My Niece's Foot, the expat band I'd joined in

Japan, trying to schedule a rehearsal for a gig or a trip to the local bar. But no: on my answering machine was the voice of The Man Himself, Noboru Tsuburaya. *Noboru Tsuburaya!* On *my* answering machine! I peeled myself off the floor and pushed shut my slack jaw. I played that message back about thirty times to make sure I'd heard him right. Was he actually asking me to call his secretary to set up a time for a job interview? *A job interview?* I made Yuka come over and listen to make sure. Yep, she said. That was exactly what he was saying.

So I went to Tokyo and had the interview. I got the tour. I even got to meet Ultraman himself (or at least a guy trying on a newly repaired Ultraman costume). And it was all I had ever imagined!

Soon after I got back from the interview in Tokyo (where I actually got to walk around in that attic full of monsters I'd seen in my Ohio dreams), I got a call telling me that not only was I hired but my salary would be about 20 percent more than the already inflated (to my mind) salary I'd asked for. Furthermore, the company would pay for half my rent in whatever apartment I chose in Tokyo. *Good googly-moogly!* What more could any human being possibly want?

For me this was like winning the lottery after being elected emperor of the whole wide world and the Playboy mansion to boot. I couldn't imagine anything better. This was heaven, absolutely and without a doubt. I had to pinch myself to make sure I wasn't dead. All my dreams had come true—granted they may have been stupid dreams, but they were mine and as of this particular Tuesday *they had all come true!*

I spent the next several months being totally blinded by my good fortune, walking around in a complete daze.

This was some weird kinda mojo for sure. How had such a thing happened? As I became aware of just how impossible it was, I started to get a little scared. In my view of the world at that point, things like this just could not possibly happen. It was utterly impossible. If I hadn't been so blinded by happiness I would have gone nuts. Maybe I did go a bit nutty. But I managed to keep it in check. Sort of.

WHENEVER I'VE REFLECTED on what happened, I am struck by the phenomenal string of coincidences that brought me to Tsuburaya. How had I just happened to pick that particular prefecture in Japan as the place to work? How had I come across that particular book in that particular book store? How had life conspired for Yuka and me to meet? How had it just so happened that I sent my letter to Tsuburaya right after the last American who worked there quit? How had I even made it to Japan in the first place? And that room full of monsters I'd dreamed of as a kid, had I somehow known I'd end up working at such a place? My head was spinning. If daffodils had flown out my ass, I couldn't have been more astounded.

I'd had a zillion jobs by then, mostly through temp agencies. As thrilled as I was, I nonetheless had an inkling that the best job in the world was still just a job. Even Johnny Ramone said that being a rock and roll guitar player was a pretty good job, but that, in the end, it also sucked just like any other job.

Yet, I knew—I just *knew*—that I had landed The Perfect Job. My life would never be dull, dreary, or disappointing again. These people got paid good money to sit around and look through *Ultraman* books, to write the scripts for *Ultraman* shows, to dress up in rubber dinosaur costumes and trash model cities! (Not to mention that there were some mind-bogglingly hot-looking babes in the sales department.)

Johnny Ramone was obviously wrong. Buddha was wrong—life wasn't suffering, life was *great!* A job at Tsuburaya Productions was definitely *not* suffering. Maybe there were people in the world who could get tired of such a life.

But not me, boy! No way in the world! This was it. Stupid as my dreams were, I had just realized them all in one bound. Maybe it was *because* my dreams were so small that I'd been able to realize them all. Whatever. I didn't want to be a rich rock and roller or movie star or dictator of a nation. Maybe I'd stumbled onto the secret for eternal happiness: Keep your dreams small and stupid.

All I knew was this was paradise on earth and nothing would ever, ever, ever change that.

Famous last words...

IF ONLY...

You may find that having is not so
pleasing a thing as wanting.
This is not logical but it is often true.

MISTER SPOCK

Rivers of sweat spilling down my forehead and into my eyes, my brain liquefying under the heat of the giant arc lamps, I rip the heavy fiberglass and latex monster mask off my head and collapse to my knees.

The skintight wetsuit transformed by the Tsuburaya Productions' costume department into the monster's silver-and-black-striped body threatens to rip open in a particularly embarrassing way. "Cut!" the director yells, no longer even bothering to hide his disgust and anger at yet another take ruined by the foreigner dressed as that transdimensional menace Alien Dada, one of Ultraman's most fearsome enemies. I fall into a useless heap on the floor while the rest of the monsters get into position for the next take.

The opening sequence of *Let's Learn English with Ultraman!* features six of Ultraman's greatest monster foes dancing behind a ten-year-old half-Japanese half-American singer named Nadia. There is a huge Ultraman live show going on the same day the shooting is scheduled, and so there aren't enough of Tsuburaya Productions' professional monster-costume actors available for the scene. I am one of a group of stupidly enthusiastic guys from the office drafted in to help finish the shoot on schedule. I'd wanted to dress up in one of those cheesy Japanese monster costumes since I was a kid but I had no idea they were so hot, stiff, and smelly. As I lie there watching the studio ceiling whirl around in crazy figure-eights over my head I wonder: How did I end up in this hell?

THAT EXPERIENCE made me wonder what else there was for me in Japan. I hadn't really done much to expand my understanding of Buddhism since coming here, although I had visited a few temples. I'd visited Eihei-ji, the temple founded in the thirteenth century by Japanese Zen's greatest teacher, Master Dogen, and seen the spot where he preached. On the whole though, Eihei-ji was nothing more than a fairly average Japanese tourist attraction—but man, it's got some big trees.

The hill leading up to the temple was lined with tacky souvenir shops selling everything from plastic Buddha statues to the requisite Ultraman toys for the kiddies. Insert 700 yen into the vending machine outside the temple and you get a ticket entitling you to walk around a cordoned-off part of the building. I didn't actually see anyone doing zazen. I didn't see anyone doing much of anything except walking around pointing at stuff and taking pictures. That was about it for my Buddhist historical explorations.

Yet I still did zazen every day at home, as I had ever since I'd started sitting with Tim, though usually just the token twenty minutes before bed. And in my first year in Japan I went to three temples to actually practice zazen. All those times had been in the form of the kind of *"Get a Taste of Zen!"* things typically organized by groups of foreigners with little involvement from the temples themselves. In one case a monk simply showed us where the zendo was then disappeared. We just saw ourselves out when we were finished doing zazen. For all I could tell the monks had all gone home by then.

Another such excursion was an overnight deal organized by some fellow JET participants at a rustic old temple high atop a mountain in a remote part of Gifu Prefecture. Still, aside from cooking and serving our meals, the temple monks were completely uninvolved.

Now that I was in Tokyo and had what could be generously described as an "open social calendar"—although it might be more accurate to call it "a severe case of being a friendless loser"—I figured it was time to get back into the Zen thing. I came across a classified ad in the local free English paper for a Zen group in Tokyo offering lectures in English and decided to take a chance. The group turned out to be called Dogen Sangha and its leader one Gudo Wafu Nishijima.

LET ME TELL YOU a little about Nishijima. Nishijima is a Zen monk who certainly doesn't fit any usual picture of what monks are supposed to be. These days, at eighty-four years old with a shaved head and the traditional monk's robes, at least he looks the part. But delve a little deeper, and the neat, easy image falls apart. Besides being a monk, Nishijima also works for a cosmetics company, a job he took after spending several years working for the Japanese Ministry of Finance.

During the early part of the Second World War, Nishijima started attending zazen sittings and lectures held by Kodo Sawaki, one of Japan's most notorious "rebel" Buddhist monks. Not content with the way Japanese Buddhism had degenerated into little more than maintaining temples as tourist attractions and hosting funerals, Sawaki wanted to return Buddhism to its fundamentals— the practice of zazen. He never had a temple of his own but wandered from place to place teaching and holding zazen sittings and so he came to be known as "Homeless" Kodo. He dispensed with most of the elaborate rituals associated with traditional Zen and stuck to a few favorite chants and bows. Fearing that Buddhism was nearly dead in Japan, he wanted to spread it beyond the Japanese islands and encouraged many of his followers to teach abroad.

In the early 1970s, Nishijima started hosting lectures on Buddhism in English at Tokyo University's Young Buddhists Association. With the help of a young British student named Mike Cross he embarked upon the massive task of translating the entirety of Master Dogen's greatest work, the *Shobogenzo,* into English—all ninety-five hefty chapters of it. Nishijima gave his group the name Dogen Sangha to signify his dedication to the teachings of Dogen but also to place a bit of conceptual distance between himself and the mainstream Soto sect of Zen Buddhism into which he'd been ordained. *Sangha,* by the way, just means a group of Buddhists. Although Nishijima received Dharma Transmission from Niwa Rempo, then the head of the Soto sect and Head Abbot of Eihei-ji, the sect's main temple, he has never felt entirely comfortable with the way they run things.

When I first started attending Nishijima's lectures, I found them infuriating. His frank arrogance was contemptible. You'd think the guy believed that no one on Earth understood Buddhism except for him. He insisted that the only Buddhist books worth reading about were Dogen's *Shobogenzo*—in his own translation, of course— and a book called *Fundamental Verses on the Middle Way,* by an ancient Indian guy named Nagarjuna. Nishijima also mentioned that all existing English translations of this latter book were totally worthless. And he had all these weird theories about the autonomic nervous system. What was a Buddhist master doing talking about medical stuff? I wanted to hear about how to reach enlightenment!

Yet for all that, I couldn't doubt this guy's sincerity. He made no effort to try to convince anyone to accept his beliefs. He simply stated them like they were undeniable facts, utterly obvious to anyone with the sense to take a look. His unstated attitude seemed to be, "You came to hear what I have to say. Well, here it is. If you don't like it, go listen to someone else."—and a lot of people did indeed walk out on him. A few times I even gave up on the guy, staying away from the lectures for weeks at a time. But after a while I'd always be back. Something about his outlook felt right to me. Something about the old man really moved me.

There's no way I can convey the full sense of what it was like to listen to him teach. Gudo Nishijima is like a force of nature. Describing his personality is like trying to describe the personality of an earthquake or a typhoon. Mostly you're not concerned about what he's really like so much as concerned about how to stay alive until he passes by. He's just a little old bald man in robes but he has this voice that can rattle walls for miles in all directions. There are times he seems to be baiting the audience to come after him, sort of like GG Allin used to do.

In case you don't know, GG Allin is perhaps the most notorious punk rocker of all time. He was so outrageous on stage that no one was really sure whether he was a performance artist nonpareil or an actual crazy person. He died in a spectacular suicide in 1993.

But Nishijima was way more dangerous than ol' GG. The punks who came to witness GG Allin swearing at them, calling them names, and hurling excrement knew they had a chance of at least beating him up with their fists if they wanted to (and many did). But Nishijima wasn't so easy to defeat. No one would think of physically attacking a kindly old monk in black robes. And no one I ever saw start an argument with him ever made it through the thing without being reduced to a sputtering fool. I know I never did.

MY UNDERWHELMING PERFORMANCE as Alien Dada wasn't my first appearance in a Japanese monster production. In 1994 I appeared as an innocent bystander dodging the laserbeam breath of the brontosaurus-like Darengelon in *Ultraman Neos*. In the film *Ultraman Zearth* I was "American News Reporter Bradley Warner," glimpsed for about three seconds reporting on the theft of a statue of King Tutankhamen by aliens. In episode one of the *Ultraman Tiga* TV series, I'm a South American member of the super-scientific team GUTS, the Global Unlimited Task Squad, reporting the sighting of a monster on Easter Island.

One of my more memorable roles occurred during episode 51 of that same TV series, in which I was cast as an American Blue Angel whose plane gets attacked by a gigantic pterodactyl-style beast devastating New York City. For this they gave me a uniform and put me into a mock-up of a cockpit complete with cast-off parts from actual planes. As I sat strapped into a pilot's chair, a guy came in and taped a bunch of little plastic bags containing explosive powder to the control panel in front of me. These charges, I was told, would be "harmless," just bright light and lots of smoke. Of course on the *Ultraman* budget they weren't about to set off any of the fireworks during the test runs. Each run-through, the guy in charge of the explosives would shout *"Bang, bang, bang!"* to cue the camera crew when to expect the explosions. Finally, everything was set. They wanted to get this in the first take—film and firecrackers cost money. I, on the other hand, was working for free.

I was to look up, yell, "The monster's too fast!" then scream as the explosives went off. I shouted my line and, right on cue, a huge fiery blast went off in my face. My scream was entirely genuine. I could feel the force of the blast and the heat on my face and chest. Amazingly, I didn't get burned—but my ears rang for the rest of the day. Later when I saw a videotape of the action, I found out that those "harmless" fireworks had created a fireball about five feet across.

That was the fun part. But it didn't take long before my dream job became—well, I won't say a *nightmare,* but it did become just a job. It was something I had to drag myself out of bed for. My paradise had melted into plain old nothing before my very eyes.

EVERY SINGLE HUMAN BEING in the world at some time thinks that "if only" this or that one of our conditions could be met then we'd be all set. "If only I had a girlfriend / boyfriend / million bucks, then I'd be happy." Or in the case of the more spiritually minded: "If only I were enlightened, then that would settle everything once and for all." Think again.

An old Chinese Zen master once said, "From birth to death it's just like this!"

Wherever you go in the world of human beings is pretty much the same. Only the details are different. All of my *gaijin* teacher friends who wanted to get out of Japan and back to the "real world" have discovered that the "real world" is hardly any different than the place they were leaving.

We always want to believe that somewhere there's a perfect situation, if only we weren't barred from it. But that's not the reality.

We always imagine that there's got to be somewhere else better than where we are right now; this is the Great Somewhere Else we all carry around in our heads. We believe Somewhere Else is out there for us if only we could find it. But there's no Somewhere Else. Everything is right here.

Maybe your lot right now could be improved. I know mine could. And working to make things better is great. But we don't *just* work to make things better and leave it at that, do we? We live in the idealized world inside our heads.

And *that* keeps us from ever really enjoying what we have right now, from enjoying the work that we're doing to create our better tomorrow. It's as if we're afraid to really commit to this moment because a better one might come along later.

This approach is totally ridiculous and completely absurd.*

AMERICANS ARE ESPECIALLY PRONE to thinking that if they can only find just the right *job*, they'll be happy. That's why we're constantly hopping from one company to another, one career to another. Most of us are realistic enough to say we know there'll be challenges wherever we go but we really do believe in our hearts that the perfect situation does exist somewhere—if only we could find it.

This belief is at the heart of all jealousy and envy, and ultimately all of our suffering. We envy the rich and powerful, we envy famous people. But their lives are just like ours. The handful of famous people I've met actually seem even *more* envious of fame than the rest of us.

Whenever I used to hear Buddhist teachers saying we shouldn't strive for money or fame I used to think it was some kind of admonition that we shouldn't have any fun. It's really not that at all. Thinking that money and fame are the keys to the perfect situation is a kind of deep confusion. Fame and money can actually stand in the way of real joy because rich people tend to get more and more easily suckered into the state of mind that *if only* they could acquire just the right house or object or lifestyle, *then* they'd be happy. Why else would movie stars and athletes who already have more money than God demand multimillion dollar contracts year after year? What could anyone possibly do with all that money? What makes even the richest,

*But life itself is absolutely hilarious, a veritable laugh riot, if you look at it the right way.

most famous and most powerful people still want more and more? In the end, what did money, power, and fame do for Kurt Cobain...or Keith Moon...or Sid Vicious...or Elvis? If this isn't a lesson that fame and money are dead-end streets, I can't imagine what else could possibly be.

My mistake was that while I could see money and fame weren't going to make everything right, I still believed that there was some *situation* where everything would be just perfect forever. By setting my sights on something truly bizarre I was no doubt trying to ensure that my dream remained forever out of reach. You read a lot these days about "fear of success" and people deliberately sabotaging their own lives in order to keep their dreams from being realized. Maybe it's not that people like this fear success so much as they fear discovering that success really isn't success at all.

We want to keep our dreams as dreams. Once we achieve our goals, when our dreams become real, we see that they aren't quite as thrilling or as fulfilling or even as interesting as we'd imagined they'd be. That can be devastating—as all the cases of rock-star ODs and CEO suicides can attest. When your dreams come true to the letter it's even harder. You can't bullshit yourself with any more *if onlys*.

Once I'd achieved my goal I had to admit to myself it wasn't what I expected and that it did not in fact make everything perfect. And this will happen to anyone who attains any kind of "success" no matter how it is defined — even if success is defined as complete, unsurpassed, perfect enlightenment. You will discover upon reaching it that whatever it is, it's not what you expected and nothing is any more perfect than it ever was.

And there is always some kind of exchange. Even breathing is a matter of exchanging one thing for another—carbon dioxide for oxygen, old breath for new, death for life and life for death. Nothing lives in any other way. When you get right down to it, most people's idea of paradise involves the equivalent of somehow just inhaling and never again breathing out.

There's no workplace in the world that's free from office politics, petty jealousies, downright stupidity. While I've never lived full-time at a Buddhist monastery, I've heard from enough people who have—both in America and Japan—to know that there's no monastery that's free of those things either. Somehow, though, when I entered Tsuburaya Productions, I managed to forget all that. I was truly surprised to rediscover the same things there that I'd found in a dozen workplaces in America. The problem was that the job itself was so like my dream of perfection that when things failed to materialize the way I'd imagined they would—the way I *knew* they should—the reality of the Buddha's first noble truth, the one misleadingly translated as, "All life is suffering," became abundantly clear.

When certain Buddhist scholars elucidate this point they usually say that even if you get what you want it's still suffering because it won't last. This isn't exactly wrong, I suppose, but to get a bit closer to the point you need to look at what suffering really is. Suffering occurs when your ideas about how things ought to be don't match how they really are. Stop for a second and look at this in your life right now. It's important.

The pain of having your dreams come true appears vividly when you realize that even if your dreams really come true, they never really come true.

From birth to death it's just like this.

SO I GRADUALLY SETTLED into doing my dream job the way I'd done every other job I'd had in my life: with care and energy but also a certain amount of detachment and boredom.

In the meantime, I played at being a real writer for Tsuburaya, not just a guy who makes up character names and promo leaflets. I submitted several stories for consideration to the *Ultraman Tiga* TV series in 1996. One of my scripts, in which the GUTS team time-travels to Japan's feudal era, was deemed interesting but too expensive to make, another in which the GUTS team become Buddhist monks and battle a monster that's not even really there was deemed just too weird. The head of the planning division liked it, but he couldn't convince the rest of the team to take on something quite that bizarre.

In 1998 when the TV series *Ultraman Gaia* was being produced, I decided to have one more go at writing an episode. The standard plot of nearly every episode is this: "Monster shows up, people try to defeat it, fail. Ultraman shows up, beats up monster, flies off into sunset." I thought it might be neat to set an episode in a parallel universe in which Ultraman is a giant bad guy who constantly attacks Earth's cities. In order to protect themselves, the earthlings create giant monsters to battle him. In this universe, the "evil" Ultraman always defeats the "good" monsters, but must fly home to recuperate before he can attack again. I wrote the story down, painstakingly translated it into Japanese with my wife's patient help, and submitted it.

I was flabbergasted when they decided to use it.

It turns out quite a lot of care goes into crafting the scripts for the *Ultraman* shows. You can do a surprising amount within the rigid format they've used for the past thirty-six years. Kinda like blues music. There are never any more than three chords in a true hardcore blues song, yet each song is unique, and after nearly a century of songwriters using those three chords, the possibilities have yet to be exhausted.

At my first meeting, Hirochiku Muraishi, the director slated for my show, asked me what my theme was. I did have a theme in mind, but I'd never expected anyone would ask me about it. I expected to be asked how many monster battles would be in the show or about how to move the action along more quickly and build to a cliffhanger before the commercial—anything but what I was trying to do with the script. My theme, I told him, was Power. It came from something Nishijima had once told me. He spotted me reading a book about Ultraman and said, "Those TV shows teach children to believe in Power."

I was pretty taken aback. I'd never thought about it but superhero shows, popular with kids all over the world, do teach children to believe in power: we are in trouble and we can't help ourselves, so someone more powerful—a superhero—has to fly in and fix our problems. And in the world of kids' TV shows he always does so out of the goodness of his heart, never asking for anything in return. Real power in the human world is not so altruistic. The only place other than in the world of superhero shows for kids where you can find powerful beings who help powerless people out and ask for nothing in return is in the sphere of religion. This is yet another way in which Buddhism is not a religion.

There's a "bodhisattva" in Buddhism called Kannon. Bodhisattvas aren't gods, supernatural beings who exist somewhere and mercifully intervene in the realm of human affairs. Nonetheless, you can ask Kannon for help. But since Buddhists do not believe in literal supernatural beings, it's understood that Kannon's help really comes from ourselves. Still, Kannon is always available to help you and will always aid you when asked.

My show was about how power can be abused. In the universe of *Ultraman*, there is always a super-scientific task force whose job it is to protect the people of Earth, and one of them has the ability to transform into Ultraman. So what if that guy went power-mad? What if he decided to use the power of Ultraman for his own gain, and what if he got the rest of his task squad to back him up? I wanted children who watched my episode to understand that their leaders are people just like themselves, and that when rotten people are given power, they do rotten things.

That went over well with Muraishi and with the show's producer, Masato Oida. What didn't go over well was my inability to write convincing dialogue in Japanese. To that end, one of our staff's pro writers, my friend Masakazu Migita, was drafted into service. The trouble started when Oida decided my story might be a little too "hard" for children. He asked that it should be made into something softer, more of a fantasy. In my draft, the alternate universe had been just like ours with a few minor changes—an expense-saving idea I'd stolen from *Star Trek*'s alternate universe episodes. It was Migita's task to make my plot more fantastical. But as he did so, the very things I'd been trying to say in my original draft got more and more muddled. By making the alternate universe clearly different from our world, the point that our own real world could just as easily go that way (albeit without the giant heroes and monsters) got lost.

Meanwhile, I'd scheduled a trip to Mexico to meet my parents, who were thinking of retiring down there. The trip had been planned and paid for long before my script had been given the green light. Going to Mexico meant that I was leaving at the crucial time when Migita was doing the final rewrites. I wasn't real happy with the version he was working on when I left, but there was little I could do. When I returned from Mexico, I found that the network had canceled our script at the last minute, even as preproduction work was being done on the show. Another writer was called in to throw together a more standard-issue *Ultraman* episode—which he pounded out in an afternoon, I'm told—and that went ahead instead.

At this point, despite the perfectness of my dream job, I realized that writing for *Ultraman* wasn't really what I wanted to do.

I'd been getting more and more involved with Nishijima's group. It was becoming clearer to me that teaching oblique Buddhist messages to kids through *Ultraman* might be okay (assuming I ever got an episode through production), but directly teaching the reality of Buddhist insights through Buddhism itself might make a whole lot more sense.

And that's what I am going to do now, in this book. Bear with it in the next chapter.

Who knows? You might like it.

THE GREAT HEART ^{OF} WISDOM SUTRA

Come on, Milhouse, there's no such
thing as a soul! It's just something
they made up to scare kids, like the
Boogie Man or Michael Jackson.
BART SIMPSON

ON THE FIRST DAY of my first Zen class at Kent, Tim read aloud a translation of the Great Heart of Wisdom Sutra and I heard the phrase "That which is form is emptiness; that which is emptiness is form." When I heard that, I knew it was right. Granted I had no idea what it *meant*, but when he came to that line I had to struggle to keep from crying.

Hearing the Heart Sutra literally changed my life. It rocked my world in many subtle and not-so-subtle ways. Maybe it'll have some kind of impact on you too. Or maybe not.

I'm going to present here the translation done by Tim's teacher Kobun Chino since that was the first one I ever heard. When a baby duck hatches, the first thing he sees, he considers to be his mother, that's called *imprinting*. In a very important way, this verse was the first thing I ever saw and so I've always considered it my mother (apologies to Mom here).

Try reading it once through without worrying too much about trying to understand it. That's the way I first heard it. There's some bizarre stuff, some arcane references and even a little bit of ancient Sanskrit. Don't worry about it. Just let the words soak in.

THE GREAT HEART OF WISDOM SUTRA

Avalokiteshvara Bodhisattva

when practicing deeply the Prajna Paramita

perceived that all five skandhas are empty

and was saved from all suffering and distress.

Shariputra, form does not differ from emptiness;

emptiness does not differ from form.

That which is form is emptiness;

that which is emptiness, form.

The same is true of feelings, perceptions, impulses,
    consciousness.

Shariputra, all dharmas are marked with emptiness;

they do not appear nor disappear,

are not tainted or pure,

do not increase or decrease.

Therefore in emptiness, no form,

no feelings, perceptions, impulses, consciousness;

no eyes, no ears, no nose, no tongue, no body, no mind;

no color, no sound, no smell, no taste, no touch,
    no object of mind;

no realm of eyes and so forth until no realm of mind-
    consciousness;

no ignorance and also no extinction of it, and so forth until
    no old age and death and also no extinction of them;

no suffering, no origination, no stopping, no path;

no cognition, also no attainment.

With nothing to attain

the bodhisattva depends on Prajna Paramita

and his mind is no hindrance.

Without any hindrance no fears exist;

far apart from every inverted view he dwells in nirvana.

In the three worlds all buddhas depend on Prajna Paramita

and attain *anuttara-samyak-sambodhi*.

Therefore know the Prajna Paramita

is the great transcendent mantra,

is the great bright mantra,

is the utmost mantra,

is the supreme mantra,

which is able to relieve all suffering

and is true not false.

So proclaim the Prajna Paramita mantra,

proclaim the mantra that says:

Gaté, gaté, paragaté, parasamgaté! Bodhi! Svaha!

Now I'll take you through it line by line.

Avalokiteshvara Bodhisattva

Avalokiteshvara, also called Guanyin or Kwan Yin in Chinese, and Kannon or Kanzeon in Japanese (and Chenrezig in Tibetan, by the way), is one of the main characters in the longer sutra from which the Great Heart of Wisdom Sutra is derived. A bodhisattva, in addition to being the subject of songs by both Steely Dan and The Beastie Boys, is a being who has vowed to put off becoming a full-fledged buddha until he (or she, but I'll stick with "he" for now—apologies again to Mom) saves all the beings in the universe. There are loads of legendary tales of Gautama Buddha's supposed previous lifetimes, and in those he is often referred to as the Bodhisattva.

In ancient Buddhism, it was a commonly held—though very much mistaken—belief that only a monk or nun could become a full-fledged buddha, and so the category of *bodhisattva*, a being devoted to freeing others rather than just attaining enlightenment for himself, was created as something regular folk could aspire to. Notice that a bodhisattva is, if you really think about it, way cooler than a buddha. It might be said that a buddha selfishly enjoys the pleasures of buddhahood while a bodhisattva puts them off until every other being in the universe enjoys them as well. Which would you rather think of yourself as?

The bodhisattva ideal became an important aspect of Mahayana Buddhism. *Mahayana* means "great vehicle." This movement was a more all-encompassing Buddhism than the monastery-bound tradition that had developed in the first centuries following Gautama Buddha's death. With the idea that regular folk could become bodhisattvas, the Mahayana sects were able to attract a greater number of followers than the older Buddhist sects, which the Mahayanists derisively called *Hinayana*, or "puny girly-man vehicle." Almost all Buddhist sects that still exist today are part of the Mahayana tradition. The notable exception is the Theravada school, which flourishes mainly in southern Asia and has recently made significant inroads into the West.

Avalokiteshvara was originally conceived of as male, but representations of him became more and more androgynous until the modern Chinese and Japanese depictions in which almost always Guanyin/Kannon is female. A Buddhist sex change!

S/he/it (!) is the bodhisattva of compassion. Compassion, mind you, isn't the same as mere love. Religions always talk about love. But to a Buddhist, love is second rate—if that. Compassion is far more important. Compassion is the ability to see what needs doing right now and the willingness to do it right now. Sometimes compassion may even mean doing nothing at all. Lots of loving people in this world go way out of their way to "try to help"—but often they do more harm than good. Stupid helpfulness is not compassion either.

Prajna Paramita

As mentioned above, this little verse is actually part of a much longer sutra. Personally I've never read the whole thing. In fact, aside from the really geeky pocket-protector academic types, you'll find that very few Buddhists have actually personally read the entire sutra. This section is called the Great Heart of Wisdom Sutra, or just the Heart Sutra for short. It's called the *heart* because it contains the core teaching of the whole sutra.

It's written in traditional Mahayana sutra–style, namely as a purported dialogue between Avalokiteshvara and Gautama Buddha's disciple Shariputra, with Gautama himself hanging out in the background meditating and only emerging toward the end of the piece to say, "Right on, bro'!"

Actually, though, it's commonly agreed by scholars that the sutra did not appear until about five hundred years after Gautama's death, and Avalokiteshvara in this context is a completely mythical character. By today's definition, we would have to classify all of the Mahayana sutras as works of fiction. This is another major point where Buddhism differs from religions. All religions firmly insist on the historical accuracy of their texts, however dubious that insistence may be. Buddhism, however, doesn't care either way. It is the meaning of the texts right here and now in our lives that is important—and that has nothing to do with mere historical veracity.

Prajna is intuitive wisdom, and it has nothing at all to do with knowledge. Prajna ain't book learnin'. The word *intuition* is used a lot these days to refer to a kind of gut feeling, and that's something like what prajna is—but it's more than that: it's a *direct knowing*. You're thinking with body and mind together. Regular thinking is only mental action, but prajna includes the physical as well.

It's also a mistake to regard prajna as emotional. Emotion itself can often be a kind of confusion. Once a feeling becomes so strong we start calling it an emotion, it's already become too powerful to deal with in any clear-eyed manner. Prajna includes feeling, but it's feeling on a more subtle level.

Think about anger. Everyone experiences a flash of anger welling up in some circumstance or other. But anger can only continue grow when it's fed by thought. Prajna is the wisdom to notice anger before it becomes a problem, to see clearly why you feel angry and what that feeling of anger really is (and is not). This goes much deeper than just saying, "I'm angry because he called me a panty-waist with carburetor breath." Why does an insult make you angry? Who is the "you" that has been insulted? What is the "you" that can get angry?

Prajna is the wisdom to get at the very root of any emotional response. Prajna is developed through the practice of zazen.

The word *paramita* essentially means "highest" (though it has other meanings as well), so in this context we simply read "prajna paramita" as the highest wisdom, the highest prajna.

Shariputra

Shariputra, as I've said, was one of Gautama Buddha's most advanced students. He was a guy with a particularly clear grasp of subtle teachings about "emptiness" (more about this concept soon)—so lots of sutras have Buddha addressing him or answering his questions. Many of the earliest sutras form the ancient Pali canon compiled after Gautama's death are almost certainly transcripts of actual talks between the two men, but in the Mahayana sutras both Gautama and Shariputra have basically become legendary figures, characters in the unfolding of a dialogue.

Five Skandhas

Buddhists do not accept the existence of a soul, some unchanging thing that is somehow "the essence" of a person. Instead they see a human being as a composite of five *skandhas*. The word *skandha* literally means "heap." Imagine a heap of junk: take away all the individual pieces of junk that make up the heap, and the heap is gone. There is no "heap essence" or "heap soul" aside from the pieces of junk on the heap. In Buddhism, the five "heaps" that make up a person are these: form, feelings, perceptions, impulses toward actions (and the actions themselves), and consciousness.

The denial of the idea of a soul is central to Buddhist understanding. Gautama Buddha was responding to the Indian idea of *atman*. This idea says that a little piece of

God, called the *atman*, exists within each one of us, and that this atman is eternally separate from the body. The Judeo-Christian idea of a soul is pretty much the same except that the soul is seen by Jews and Christians as being eternally separate not just from the physical body but from God as well. It can go hang out with God, but can never merge into God as can the atman in the Hindu view.

Gautama Buddha looked carefully and exhaustively and could see no reason to accept the permanent existence of anything that could be called self or soul or atman. This is the basis of the teaching of *anatman*, "no self"—which has been verified by generation after generation of Buddhists for 2,500 years.

Nothing in the universe is permanent—and the thing we call "self" is no different.

Form Is Emptiness
Emptiness is the single most misunderstood word in all of Buddhism. The original Sanskrit word for this is *shunyata*, which ultimately points to the as-it-is-ness of things, the state of things being as they are without being colored by our views and ideas. But really, no matter how you define this word, it is still used to express something for which there simply were and are no adequate words, definitions, or concepts. The set of tools we're given to write about Buddhism are simply not up to the task. Nor were they up to the task 2,500 years ago.

Emptiness is not a nihilistic concept of voidness. Emptiness is not meaninglessness. Emptiness is that condition which is free from our conceptions and our perceptions. It's the world as it is before we come along and start complaining about the stuff we don't like.

Nishijima translates the famous line "Form is emptiness, emptiness is form," as, "Matter is the immaterial, the immaterial is matter." John Lennon expressed the same idea in *Everybody's Got Something to Hide Except for Me and My Monkey:* "Your inside is out and your outside is in." The world we perceive and the thing that perceives the world are one and the same. Another modern Indian teacher, a guy named Krishnamurti, was fond of saying, "The observer is the observed."

This all sounds pretty weird to most people when they begin studying Buddhism; it sounds so bizarre as to seem meaningless. But it is really a very concrete statement. It may, in fact, be the most concrete, most clear statement you can possibly make.

This book is you, you are this book. Reality is you, you are reality.

It's like the scene in David Cronenberg's movie *The Fly.* Having subjected himself to a scientific experiment involving teleportation, Professor Brundle (played by Jeff Goldblum) gets his molecular structure combined with that of a fly that gets into the machinery. Brundle becomes progressively more and more flylike, both physically and mentally. As he comes to terms with this, even begins to revel in it, he starts referring to himself as "Brundlefly." He understands the two—fly and Brundle—are really one, but language can't handle that concept. Same deal here. It's not "you" and "the universe." It's "universeyou."

The matter of matter and its relationship to mind is one of the most interesting aspects of Buddhism. Buddhist ideas about mind and matter are at once very much at odds with most Western philosophy, as well as the "commonsense" interpretation, and also similar in many ways to the notions being expressed recently by cutting-edge physicists and neuroscientists.

I recently read an article in the *Chicago Tribune* called "All in Your Head" by science writer Ronald Kotulak. In it, he says, "The starting point for consciousness may be the universe, which many physicists believe is made of information. The things we see as matter and energy are really information being transformed from one state to another." The human brain can't deal with all the information available, the article continues, so it transforms sensory input into what scientists call neural correlates of consciousness (or in the lingo, NCCs), symbolic forms that it can work with more easily.

He goes on to quote Piero Scaruffi, a lecturer at Caltech, who says, "Consciousness is no more magic than electricity. We can study consciousness if we can study the particles that give rise to it." In effect what Scaruffi is saying is simply, "emptiness is form." But the understanding that form is emptiness seems to elude him—as it does most scientists.

In the same article Kotulak mentions that in order for scientists to investigate consciousness, "They must first work their way through the thicket of the unconscious mind. It sees things before we are aware of them. We duck a surprise blow, jump out of the way of a speeding car.... Some experts estimate that 90 percent of the brain's workings are at the unconscious level." In fact, as neuroscience is beginning to realize, we can never really separate the conscious and unconscious.

Science is at the verge of understanding the problem, yet, by and large scientists are unable to make the intuitive leap that Gautama Buddha made millennia ago to see how to resolve the contradiction. As a culture we're beginning to see that we cannot comprehend the universe through the symbols of the conscious mind alone.

Yet the idea that the practice of zazen can directly allow a true understanding of the universe to emerge is somehow too strange for Western science and philosophy to come to grips with. It seems too mystical, too weird. The insights to be had through the long, boring practice of zazen, though, are available to anyone at all who commits to the practice—

including you. These insights have been empirically confirmed by the process of Dharma Transmission from teacher to student for thousands of years.

"Dharma Transmission" sounds like fanatical religious conversion, doesn't it? Maybe even brainwashing: Your teacher believes it, you listen to him long enough and you begin to believe it too. But seeing reality is not a matter of absorbing a set of beliefs that have been handed down to you.

Here's an analogy (it's a little far-fetched but the point is there, so bear with me): Imagine a person who's been blind since birth suddenly gaining the ability to see. Now the formerly blind person and any sighted person can immediately and directly agree that, for instance, oak leaves in summer are basically the same color as grass. But another blind person listening might assume that they'd just arbitrarily agreed upon a shared, groundless belief. A real Buddhist teacher is like someone who is no longer blind. Practicing zazen is like gradually (or maybe not so gradually) getting your sight back. Dharma Transmission is what happens when your sight clears enough that you can see what your teacher and the Buddha have already seen: things as they are.

The major difference between the ideas proposed by scientists and those proposed by Buddhists stems from the fact that scientists want to understand things through analytical thought alone. Buddhists realize that any true understanding of the relationship between mind and matter must include intuitive understanding that involves the whole mind—conscious and subconscious—as well as the body and ultimately every piece of the universe itself.

This kind of understanding cannot be expressed symbolically in words used in the usual way. To the extent that it can be expressed symbolically, the phrase "Form is emptiness, emptiness is form" really is as clear as it gets.

Suffering, Origination, Stopping, Path

This phrase represents the four noble truths outlined by Gautama Buddha in his first talks after his own enlightenment experience. The usual understanding is that the first truth is that all life suffers. Gautama Buddha actually used the word *dukkha*, a word in the Pali language meaning something more like "unsatisfactory experience." The second noble truth is traditionally interpreted as saying that the origination of suffering is desire. The third truth is usually understood to say that stopping desire leads to the stopping of suffering. The fourth is the truth of the Right Way, usually given in the form of the noble eightfold path, which leads to the stopping of desire. The eight "folds" are these: right understanding, right thought, right speech, right action, right livelihood, right effort, right mindfulness, and right concentration.

Lemme give you my takes on these truths.

The first noble truth, suffering, represents idealism. When you look at things from an idealistic viewpoint everything sucks, as The Descendents said in the song called "Everything Sucks" (from the album *Everything Sucks*). Nothing can possibly live up to the ideals and fantasies you've created. So we suffer because things are not the way we think they ought to be. Rather than face what really is, we prefer to retreat and compare what we're living through with the way we think it oughta be. Suffering comes from the comparison between the two.

Even physical suffering works like this. I saw this fact clearly for myself about a year ago when I passed a kidney stone, allegedly the most painful experience a person can actually survive. I don't know about that, but I can tell you that the pain was *astoundingly* bad. And yet when I stopped comparing what I thought I ought to feel like (namely, free from pain) to what I actually felt like (namely, in *enormous* pain), things became far better. It still hurt like hell, don't get me wrong. But if you're not trying to run away from the unavoidable hell of suffering, if you just let it be, your whole experience is transformed utterly. The Buddhist author and nun Pema Chödron calls this transformation "the wisdom of no escape."

This leads to the second noble truth, the origination of suffering: our wish that things be different from what they are when they cannot possibly be. Things can never be other than they are. This moment can never be other than it is. So the "desire" often spoken of by Buddhist teachers isn't just the fact that we desire that big car or that busty redhead with the nose-ring or that hunky guy who delivers for Domino's®. Everyone has desires. We can't live without them. Nor should we. The problem isn't that we have natural desires and needs. It's that we have a compulsive (and ultimately stupid!) desire for our lives to be something other than what they actually are. We have a world in our minds that we call "perfect" and a world in front of us (and within us) that can't possibly match that image. The problem is the way we let our desires stand in the way of our enjoyment of what we already have.

Is this confusing? The world within can be quite distinct from what out brain wants it to be. The brain is often in conflict with itself. You're depressed but you want to be happy. You're horny but you want to have self-control. You're scatterbrained but you want to be focused.

The second noble truth was never supposed to be taken to mean our natural desires are evil and should be eliminated. Gautama had already tried that path as a ascetic yogi. After trying to abstain from all of his desires (including the desire to eat), he found himself thin and weak and miserable—and no closer to enlightenment than he had been when he started out (although he was way closer to Corpseville). He broke his fast by accepting a bowl of rice from a milkmaid who was taking it to a temple as an offering to one of the gods. Only after acknowledging and accepting his natural human desire for food and regaining his natural strength was he able to embark upon the practice that culminated in his enlightenment. Such a person would not be likely to preach that natural desire itself is the cause of suffering.

The third noble truth, stopping suffering, represents action in the present moment. It's not that we force ourselves to stop having desires. That wouldn't solve anything and it's impossible anyhow. Trying to force yourself not to desire just brings up more desires (not the least of which is the desire not to desire). You'll often hear religious-type people saying, "The only thing that I desire is desirelessness." Sinead O'Connor has an album called *I Do Not Want What I Haven't Got*. The only state in which you don't want what you don't have is *death*. Maybe Sinead was trying to start a "Sinead is dead" rumor....

You desire a Jaguar XKR but you've got a Chevy Shitbox (this is a car Chevy made awhile ago—it wasn't very popular at the time, but a lot of people drive them now). When you want to go to the supermarket, what makes more sense: sitting there and wishing you had that Jag or getting in your Shitbox and actually driving? If you have desires, leave them as they are and do what needs to be done. Maybe you wish you'd bought that new Ken Wilber book instead of this one. Well, there's no accounting for taste, but this is what you spent your money on so you may as well finish it.

Ultimately, the noble eightfold path is reality itself. To act according to the noble eightfold path is to act in accordance with reality. And that's all.

The Three Worlds
The three worlds are the past, present, and future.* This is a common Buddhist expression that seems to throw a lot of

. . . .
*Or: matter, volition, and nonmatter. Take your pick.

people. They think it's some kind of reference to Other Realms or higher states of consciousness or some such crap.

The past and the future—even the present—are just inventions by the conscious mind for dealing with reality in an organized way. They're symbolic representations. And representations aren't reality.

We'll never find the past and future no matter where we look. Nor will we find the present—but let's put that one aside for a couple of minutes. On my desk is a picture of my nephew when he was five dressed up as Gammera, the famous Japanese fire-breathing giant turtle. He's twelve now and no longer dresses up as Gammera. That five-year-old in the picture can never be found. In one sense the past exists since the state of our own bodies and minds is the accumulation of past actions. But even this past exists only now.

We usually believe that the past creates memory. Real events occurred in the real past and we remember them—but in fact that's only half the truth. The other half, every bit as important, is that memory creates the past. We are actively constructing our own past right now every bit as much as we create our own future. We can look at dramatic examples, but it's true in mundane ways as well.

Was Thomas Jefferson a brave champion of human freedom or an exploitative slave-owner who enjoyed a bit on the side with his female property? History is rewritten constantly—and the "past" changes. Stalin reshaped the past by erasing his enemies from official photographs and we are constantly revising our own pasts in more subtle, but ultimately quite similar, ways.

Furthermore, our perceptions of events at the time they are happening is always flawed and incomplete and then we reshape those flawed perceptions every time we revisit those memories. The past exists only in our minds and our minds are easily changeable and so the past itself becomes malleable as well.

There's another Buddhist sutra called the Diamond Sutra—*diamond* because its wisdom cuts through anything. The Diamond Sutra says, "The mind of the past is unknowable, the mind of the future is unknowable, the mind of the present is unknowable." The mind of the past is unknowable because the past is not where you are. Ever. You cannot find your past no matter where you search. Ultimately that concept we call "the past" is little more than a clever fiction to explain how things got the way they are now—and sometimes this fiction doesn't even explain things all that well.

We may long to revisit the past, but we really never can. And all those idyllic memories we have, well, we know deep down things probably weren't quite as rosy as we like to remember them (or as wholly and utterly bad, if that's the way our memories tend to go).

The mind of the future is unknowable. As a guy who collects a lot of weird stuff, I run up against this one a lot. I'll sometimes see a certain old monster book or something at a price that's just a little bit too steep. So I'll sit there and wonder, "Will I regret it later if I don't buy this now?" Of course, you can't answer that question. People stress themselves out all the time over variations of the same question. If I sign this contract, will it make my company big money? If I ask her out for a date, will she say yes? And if she says yes, will I end up enjoying the date or regretting it? You don't know what the future will be. You might take on an awful job in order to make a lot of money "for the future" but what if you drop dead before then? You never know. Of course, you need to think about the future to some extent. I wouldn't write a book without imagining a future time when it might be read. But don't get too hung up on the future. The future's out of your control. Enjoy what's happening right now. Do what is appropriate, what is right, in the present moment and let the future be the future.

So what about that present moment? The Diamond Sutra tells us that the mind of the present is unknowable. What's that mean? We think we know the mind of the present—after all, here it is! But we don't really know it. We can't really see it.

Wholly in the midst of something, you can't possibly see it. As I write this my eyes look at the keyboard (if I'd learned to type correctly, they'd be watching the screen) but I can't see my own eyes anymore than I can bite my teeth. I can only see their reflection and experience their effects. Trying to see one's present mind is just like that. I can only see the reflection of my mind in the universe or in my own past.

The present moment is the razor's edge of time, slicing through both future and past like a red-hot machete through a stick of I-Can't-Believe-It's-Not-Butter.™ Buddhist writings sometimes refer to *mind-moments*, the conceptually shortest possible division of time. It's said that there are sixty-four mind-moments in a finger snap. I couldn't care less whether this has any scientific value in modern terms—it's just a poetic attempt to illustrate the fleetingness of the present moment. In the present moment there isn't even time to complete a single thought, no matter how simple. In the present moment not even perception has time to occur. Action alone exists.

And yet this fleeting teeny-weeny present moment is the *only* time in which you are free to act. The reality of the unkowable past is set. Done and gone. Our ability to mentally manipulate it is an illusion. Yet in this moment, our past actions affect our life here and now. Within the confines in which our past action has placed us, we are *absolutely free* right now. That's an important point—make sure you see it.

The future is not here. Completely unattainable. Yet in this moment, the action we take affects our and the universe's future circumstances infinitely and unknowably. Here and now we can do something real.

Everything exists in this moment. This moment is the basis of all creation. The universe wasn't created the Biblical six thousand years ago or even the scientific fifteen billion. The universe is created *right now* and *right now* it disappears. Before you even have time to recognize its existence, it's gone forever. Yet the present moment penetrates all of time and space. In Dogen's words, "What is happening here and now is obstructed by happening itself; it has sprung free from the brains of happening."

In other words, we can't know the present in the usual sense because the present is obscured by the present itself and by the act of perceiving it and conceiving of it. Form meets emptiness here and now and all of creation blossoms into being.

Nirvana

Betcha think I'm gonna make some reference to Kurt Cobain's band. That's not the real Nirvana. The real Nirvana was a two-man band from England who put out some great psychedelic LPs in the '60s. But that's not what the Heart Sutra is talking about.

In the West, nirvana is often misunderstood as some kind of Buddhist heaven, or, since *nirvana* literally means "cessation" or "extinction," a lot of people have a seriously mistaken tendency to equate the idea with nihilism. Others equate nirvana with some kind of everlasting spiritual bliss. Nirvana isn't about bliss. If you want bliss, you'd be better off smokin' a fat ol' doobie, dude. Just brace yourself for a stiff dose of reality again when you've used up yer stash.

If you must, you can understand nirvana as a kind of goal of Buddhist practice. Now, any good Buddhist teacher will tell you it's the *path* that's important in Buddhism and not the goal. It's like shooting at a target with a bow. You just aim as well as you can and let the sucker fly. Maybe you hit, maybe you don't. Either way, you do what this moment calls for. And this one. And this one. In *Fundamental Verses of the Middle Way*, our old Indian buddy Nagarjuna says that nirvana is not reality. I agree but I'll add that nirvana is also *ultimate* reality. Buddhism's just chock full o' contradictions. Doncha love it?

And here's something that'll really get your panties in a bunch: Maybe your concept of ultimate reality has no counterpart in ultimate reality.

Anuttara-samyak-sambodhi

This means "complete, unsurpassed, perfect enlightenment." Notice, though, that the sutra first says the bodhisattva has nothing to attain and that, *because of having nothing to attain*, he attains complete liberation. You can't attain liberation the way you can attain a 1968 Camaro or a D-plus on a math test. You can only attain liberation by clearly seeing *there is nothing to attain*.

Complete liberation sounds like a big deal. And it is. It's the biggest deal around. But don't make too much of it—because it's also absolutely nothing at all.

I love the covers of those New Age books that show some Enlightened Saint with blue halos around his body, shining pure white light from his head and fingertips. It's pure crap. A real enlightened being doesn't look any different from anyone else. They're just ordinary people like you. That other stuff's just special effects. *Annutara-samyak-sambodhi* is you. Enlightenment is reality itself.

And reality is you—naked, stinky, and phony as all get-out.

Reality doesn't know a damned thing.

Reality has doubts and insecurities.

Reality gets horny sometimes and sometimes reality likes to read the funny papers.

Reality is an old guy in Cleveland Heights complaining that his grandkids have stolen his dentures again.

Reality is five guys trying to tune three guitars and a Farfisa compact organ to the same pitch and failing miserably.

Reality is the source of every star, every planet, every galaxy; every dust mote, every atom; every klepton, lepton, and slepton.

Reality is the basis of every booger up your nose, every pit-stain in your dad's T-shirts, and every dingleberry on your ass.

Reality is this moment.

The Great Transcendent Mantra
The last section is really different from the rest and seems to be encouraging us to chant that little line at the end, *"Gaté, gaté, paragaté, parasamgaté. Bodhi! Svaha!"* (*Gaté* is pronounced "gah-tay," by the way.) This basically means "Gone, gone, all the way gone to the other shore. Enlightenment! Hot damn!" It's not really meant to be chanted. It's just an expression of joy in response to realization.

Someone once asked Kobun Chino, who was another student of Nishijima's teacher, what that line meant, and Kobun replied, "I don't know, that's just Indian stuff."

A lot of Buddhism is wrapped up with Indian spiritual traditions. But that's not the important part. Woody Allen often exclaims *"Jesus!"* in his movies but that doesn't mean he's a Christian. The mantra at the end of the piece is just a motif that was common in the culture at the time it was written.

"The other shore" is enlightenment but enlightenment is also this shore, where we are right now.

Does that irk ya? No? Read it again until it does.... If Zen Buddhism were only the understanding that what we are right now is fine and dandy why do we bother practicing zazen and reading books and listening to teachers? It's an important question.

This was the burning question that our man Dogen—the founder of Japanese Soto Zen and one of the coolest Zen guys ever—took up when he began pursuing Buddhism in earnest: If we're already perfect as we are, why should we study Buddhism and practice Zen? No one could answer Dogen's question for him, and so Dogen had to find the truth for himself. In a sense, Dogen's entire multivolume *Shobogenzo* was his attempt to answer this one simple-sounding question. But that's his answer. What's yours?

There are people who think of the spiritual life as a journey. Buddhism isn't like that. We may use the word *path*, but we're not trying to get anywhere. We're trying to fully experience the wonder and perfectness of being right here. Some of those other paths might claim to whisk you off to some magical place—and maybe they'll really do it. But when you get there you'll be just as baffled as you are right now.

BUDDHISM WON'T GIVE YOU THE ANSWER. Buddhism might help you find your own right *question*, but you've gotta supply your own answers. Sorry. No one else's answer will ever satisfy you—nor should it. But the real magic is that once you have your own true answer, you'll find you're not alone. As unique as your own true answer is—the one you find after questioning and questioning and questioning—it will be absolutely in tune with the answer Gautama Buddha found all those centuries ago, the answer Nagarjuna expounded upon, the answer Bodhidharma brought to China, and the one that Dogen wrote about in Japan.

And *that* answer will announce itself like thunder from the sky overhead and an earthquake from the ground beneath your feet. And it will be just like nothing at all.

Sitting in the back of your grandma's VW Bug, in that little indentation there by the rear window, you're three years old and the world is big. Suddenly, as the engine warms up and the car begins to back down the driveway, you look out at the clear blue sky and for an instant see that you are everything. You want to say something, but none of the words you have will stick at all; nothing will come except for a wide, wide smile that crosses all of space and time—and the moment is utterly forgotten. Then one day you're walking along the banks of a river somewhere far, far from that driveway and all at once it comes rushing back, though it never really left.

But still, none of the words you have will stick to it at all.

"DON'T WORRY, IT WILL COME...
WITH ENLIGHTENMENT!"

Reality is that which, when you stop
believing in it, doesn't go away.
PHILIP K. DICK

WHILE LIVING IN TOKYO and working on selling Ultraman to the world, I kept attending Nishijima's weekly zazen sittings, finding them alternately stimulating and exasperating.* The nice little Zen books on the shelves these days don't give you much of a sense of how truly grating Zen masters can be. They're the ultimate in know-it-alls. You can't tell them anything. And Nishijima may be the very worst of the lot. He seems to delight in throwing lines into his talks that are guaranteed to put everyone in the room on edge. The image of the gentle Zen master soothing his audience with tranquil words of serenity and peace is a Hollywood invention that far too many wanna-bes spend far too much energy learning to imitate. Nishijima's talks are never stilling—they're downright irritating.

In addition to his weekly sittings and lectures, Nishijima also hosts several zazen retreats at a temple near the city of Shizuoka, in the foothills of Mount Fuji about two hours south of Tokyo by bullet train. It's a beautiful old Zen temple surrounded by tea fields, miles from the nearest con-

---

*Much like I imagine you're finding this book.

venience store and not a McDonald's® or Starbucks® in sight. Still, if you desperately need a sugar-laden soft drink, you can take a five minute walk down the hill to the vending machine out in front of the little noodle shop that caters to tourists who stop by the temple and folks who come around to arrange funerals.

As far as I could tell during my first visit the main activities of the monks at the temple seemed to be hanging out in the kitchen watching vapid TV chat shows, drinking beer and brushing up on the chants used in funeral services. Over the next few years I discovered I was pretty off base with that assessment. The guy I'd seen drinking all the beer turned out not to be one of the monks (though he did have a shaved head and lived in a temple—sue me for getting that one wrong) and managed to give up the booze by the following summer—no small feat in Japan where you can get plastered seven nights a week and still not be considered an alcoholic. The monks are in fact all hard-working guys who perform an important service for their community. Still, apart from the head of the temple who usually joins us for at least one sitting, the only other monk there I've ever seen doing zazen—which is the central practice of Zen Buddhism, mind you—was a Sri Lankan guy from the Theravada school of Buddhism who was there as part of some Buddhist exchange program. Unfortunately, this is pretty typical of Buddhist temples all over Japan.

Nishijima's retreats are pretty lightweight as Zen retreats go. While many such retreats have their students wake up at 3 o'clock in the morning, Nishijima lets his students get up at a very leisurely 4:30. There are four zazen periods each day, two of which are forty-five minutes while the other two are an hour and a half each (that's forty-five minutes of zazen, fifteen minutes of walking meditation, and another forty-five minutes of zazen). This is about half, if that, of what the really rigorous temples make their students do.

The retreats are just three days long, rather than the week-long or even month-long affairs elsewhere. Still, if you've never done that kind of thing before, even this can be a major jolt to the system.

BY THE TIME I went to my first formal retreat, I'd already been doing zazen for eleven years and going to Nishijima's lectures for two. But my first retreat with Nishijima was my first experience in an actual temple with an actual Japanese Zen priest running the show.

I hated it.

For starters I was completely confused about the arrangements. Bonehead that I am, rather than signing on for the annual English-language retreat for foreigners, I signed on for the one Nishijima holds for new members of the company he works for. The company president is enamored of zazen and requires all new employees to attend one of these. A bunch of spotty-faced new college grads who've just entered the fabulously exciting cosmetics industry are herded up to the mountains to sit still for three tedious days. There's no beer, no dried-fish snacks, no karaoke or party games—just peace and solitude and sitting up straight facing a wall all weekend long. Needless to say these kids are not happy campers.

I ended up being one of three of Nishijima's special guests that weekend, along with Jeremy Pearson, one of his long-time students, and a strange Korean man who was apparently some kind of philosophy professor somewhere. The four of us shared a room on the temple's second floor.

I didn't know Jeremy very well at the time, but he had a shaved head, knew every chant and mealtime ritual, and wore a set of monk's robes all weekend. Clearly he was a very serious Zen guy. I never could work out exactly why the Korean guy was there. He spoke fluent English and could get by moderately in Japanese, and he had obviously studied a lot of Buddhist literature and considered himself quite the expert in the field. For all I knew he might have been one of Korea's most renowned Buddhist scholars. He certainly carried himself like Korea's most renowned *something*. Maybe he had come to get a bit of hands-on experience with Japanese Zen, no doubt so that he could go back to Korea and legitimately claim to have been through some real Japanese-style Zen training.

But my main impression of him was this: He farted a lot.

Now don't get me wrong, of course passing gas is fine and normal and natural. But this man seemed to have no idea that doing so loudly and odoriferously in the middle of a polite conversation was potentially a bit off-putting. He'd just be chattering away then lift a cheek and let one rip without the slightest pause in his speech. I'd heard about some Asian countries where nose-picking in public is not considered odd or rude, but I don't think there's any part of the world where farting is considered an ordinary part of polite social intercourse—and Japan *certainly* is not such place. The man had a lot of the qualities of the autistic people I used to work with when I'd been an instructor at the Summit County Board of Mental Retardation. He seemed unaware that there were other people in the world. He spoke only in monologues as if he'd created his own mental images of people and reacted to those images rather than the people themselves. Before he asked you a question, he already had your answer worked out in his mind and no matter what answer you actually gave, he responded to the one he'd heard in his mind. It made for some very odd conversations. Something like this:

> FARTING MAN: What's your favorite color?
> ME: Blue.
> FARTING MAN: You know red is a symbol of...
> *(blah-blah-blah about red for an hour)*

Okay, I'm exaggerating a little—but not much.

Anyhow, I arrived at this particular retreat with a chip on my shoulder. I'd been doing zazen for over a decade by then and I was pretty miffed that I had yet to reach enlightenment. I'd read all the major Buddhist sutras and had made a thorough study of most of the major Indian holy books. I had shelves full of dog-eared books by big-wig spiritual teachers like Krishnamurti, Ramana Maharshi, Shunryu Suzuki, and anybody else who'd written on the subject of being enlightened. I'd even been to Christian churches to check out their ideas about "born-again experiences," which I figured might have been a kind of Christian version of enlightenment. (They weren't. FYI.) Buddy, if anyone shoulda been enlightened it was me!

One evening, I was upstairs with Nishijima, Jeremy, and Farting Man, and I steeled up my nerves enough to ask Nishijima about enlightenment.

Let me give you a bit of background. In a nutshell there are two major schools of Zen in Japan: Soto, to which Nishijima belonged and in which my teacher Tim McCarthy had studied and taught; and the Rinzai school, Soto's main competitor, as it were. The difference between them is this: the Rinzai school believes in enlightenment and the Soto school doesn't.

All right, admittedly it's a good bit more complex and interesting than that. But for now, that's all you need to know to follow the story.

Knowing that Nishijima was a Soto guy, I was trying to be cool about the whole enlightenment thing. I didn't actually use the *e*-word, I just kinda hinted around, saying stuff like "I've been studying for ten years and I still haven't *got it*, you know? I mean I don't, like, y'know, *understand anything...*"—everything short of nudging and winking to show him I was in on the big secret.

So at this point Farting Man piped in, in a fatherly tone,

like a learned Oxford don: "Don't worry, it will come...,"
he said, smiling broadly, *"with enlightenment!"* I'm sure
he would have patted me on the knee if I hadn't sat myself
a safe distance away to avoid being gassed.

"Don't say that!" Jeremy snapped. "That's not it at all!"

This reprimand made absolutely no impression on Farting
Man, who continued to smile beatifically. I'm not sure he
even heard it. Judging by the smug, satisfied smile on his
face, what he'd heard must have been something like, "Yea
brother, verily you speak the truth which this young one
has yet to meet."

Nishijima himself ignored all this and tried his best to
explain the problem to me. I don't recall what he said but it
didn't clear anything up for me. I listened respectfully and
asked a few questions but he seemed to be talking in circles.

ENLIGHTENMENT is probably the single most written-about
subject in all of Buddhism. But it's a damn tricky subject.
In Philip Kapleau's famous book *The Three Pillars of Zen*
there are several descriptions of people's "enlightenment
experiences." This was a bold move on Kapleau's part,
since such experiences are generally considered "secret"
and not appropriate for talking about, and had rarely been
published up until then. In that book there were stories of
guys watching the sky open up and start laughing with
them, and there were tears and shouts and drama all over
the damn place. This was one of the first books I read about
Zen, so I walked around for the first year or two of practicing zazen waiting for the moment when something like
that would happen to me. Once, while strolling around the
campus of Kent State University, I thought I'd got it. I just
suddenly got all giddy and laughed like an imbecile at
everything. Later I talked to Tim, my Zen teacher at the
time, saying stuff like, "Y'know, was that, like, um...*it*?"—
again carefully avoiding the *e*-word. Nope, he'd said, laugh-

ing like an idiot was just something that beginners in Zen sometimes did. *Beginner?!* I'd been practicing for almost two whole years, dammit!

By the time I ended up at Nishijima's retreat, though, I'd had eight more years of practice. For the year or so prior to that retreat I'd even been pretty good about practicing. I was starting to believe in it again for some reason. But zazen is a pretty hard thing to believe in since the results appear so slowly. In fact, I'd be inclined to tell you these days that the results never appear at all. Well, it isn't that there aren't any results. Not exactly. The problem is in the concept of what constitutes a "result." But let's not go there just now.

I've met people who've fallen ass-over-teakettle in love with zazen after only a day or two, maybe even one lecture. Those people always strike me as airheads, the kind of goof-balls who could just as easily go for crystal healing or angels. Enthusiasm is fine but too much is never a good thing. Folks who get too hot on zazen right at the beginning rarely stick with it long. Pretty soon the fervor cools, the crush passes, and they lose interest. Me, I *hated* zazen from the start and still do sometimes. I did it the way people go on diets or give up smoking. It sucked, but I could tell it was somehow good for me. Hating zazen, on the other hand, is no impediment to coming to real understanding. In fact it's a time-proven method.

In my years of zazen nothing like what was written in Kapleau's book had ever happened to me. I kept waiting and waiting, but no dice. There's an old Zen tale about a monk who got enlightened when he heard the sound of a pebble hitting a tile. So every time I heard a sharp little sound like that I'd think, "Okay! Maybe I'll get it right now. Wait for it, wait for it—.... Nope. Nuthin'. *Crap!*"

REALLY THOUGH, I've come to see it's useless to talk about "enlightenment" at all. Our man Dogen said it best by saying that *zazen itself* is enlightenment. For a long time I hated that statement with a real passion: *Yeah, right! Sitting in zazen is pain and boredom, that's what it is.* It's your head hitting the wall in front of you when you can't fight off sleep any longer. It's your brain full of thoughts so asinine you hate to believe they're really yours. It's feeling like your knees are going to seize up permanently at any second and thinking you'll never walk again. It's looking at your watch when you thought you'd been going for a solid twenty minutes and finding out you've only been at it for three. If that's enlightenment, I thought, then maybe I signed up for the wrong course.

For everyone—*everyone*—who first takes it up, zazen is tedious and awful. Your brain is in constant motion like there's a hive of angry wasps in your head. There are moments when you're certain you're going to have to leap right off your cushion and run around the room singing the chorus of *Hello, Dolly!* just to keep from going utterly bananas. Anybody who doesn't feel that way about it, at least sometimes, is not doing the practice very sincerely. Zazen isn't about blissing out or going into an alpha brainwave trance. It's about facing who and what you really are, in every single goddamn moment. And you aren't bliss, I'll tell you that right now. You're a mess. We all are.

But here's the thing: that mess is itself enlightenment. You'll eventually see that the "you" that's a mess isn't really "you" at all. But whether you notice your own enlightenment or not is utterly inconsequential; whether you think you're enlightened or not has nothing to do with the real state of affairs.

We all have a self-image and we call that self-image "me." I do. You do. Dogen did and so did Gautama Buddha. Their enlightenment didn't change the fact that they had a self-image. Nor did they stop referring to that image as "me" when trying to communicate to someone else. Obviously you can't talk about anything at all without socially accepted and understood words to use to refer to it. The problem with our self-image is that we don't see it for what it really is: a useful fiction. The idea that our self-image is something permanent and substantial is so basic to us that we would probably never even think to question it. We *believe* in it; we believe that because it's such a useful fiction it's really real. It may be the *only* thing most of us actually believe in. The truth comes when you can see that your self-image is just a convenient reference point and nothing more, and that you as you had imagined yourself do not exist.

This is another way Buddhism differs from religion. Every religion in the world starts off from the premise that the self is a substantial entity and builds from there. They all start off on a foundation that isn't just wobbly, it's entirely absent! It's like trying to build a house by stacking bricks in the sky.

I'd been searching for enlightenment for all those years without realizing that the "I" who wanted to be enlightened wasn't real. I was looking at the problem in completely the wrong way. I was expecting some great change to happen to "me." It doesn't work that way at all. But nor is it the case that realizing the self isn't real somehow destroys you. In the *Shobogenzo* Dogen says, "Realization doesn't destroy the individual any more than the reflection of the moon breaks a drop of water. A drop of water can reflect the whole sky."

SO I SPENT THE FIRST NIGHT at that temple avoiding Farting Man and being baffled by what Nishijima said about enlightenment, then it was time for bed. Just as I was about to roll over for the second half of a good night's sleep, there came a tremendous clanging, like cold ice picks being driven into my ears. The kid with the thankless job of doing the morning wake-up ritual was making the rounds of the temple shaking a noisy brass bell. This is what passes for a friendly call from the reception desk in Zen. Nishijima was up and folding his futons in seconds, with Jeremy quickly following suit. Farting Man yawned, stretched, then got to work on folding his up too. I lingered in bed a bit longer trying to fend off the inevitable but gave up after the rest of them had stepped over me a few times.

I went through the rest of the retreat remaining thoroughly unenlightened. Farting Man remained oblivious. And Jeremy remained, well, bald and Buddhist-looking. But I was pleased when once, after Farting Man left the room, Nishijima whispered to me and Jeremy, "You know, he is a very strange man."

It would take several more years of struggle and frustration before I got any glimmer as to what the answer to the whole enlightenment question might be, or to even properly understand the question itself. I'd formed a pretty clear image of what enlightenment ought to feel like and I kept waiting for that image to become reality. Unsurprisingly, it never did. Now I'm sure it never will.

D.T. SUZUKI, the first really popular Zen Buddhist writer in the Western world was a Rinzai man all the way. His books are chock full of references to *satori*, the Japanese word for enlightenment. Rinzai teachings stress the importance of enlightenment experiences and students in the Rinzai school strive very hard to achieve them. The Soto school has a completely different view of the subject.

A lot of Soto school Zen teachers refuse to even talk about "enlightenment." It's pointless, they'll tell you. All it does is muddle the issue. The Soto view is that these so-called enlightenment experiences just aren't really all that and a bag o' chips. And yet Soto teachers do acknowledge there is *something*, a kind of experience that eventually occurs and that has been mistakenly and misleadingly called "enlightenment." Nishijima likes to call it "solving the philosophical problems." Sometimes, if you catch him in a good mood, he'll call it "*second* enlightenment." The first enlightenment is, of course, zazen.

The experience that Nishijima calls solving the philosophical problems is undeniably real—but it should not be overemphasized or overvalued. A lot of people have the idea that enlightenment will be a kind of retirement from life. They figure that once they get it, everything will just flow easily and they'll never have to make any more effort. They look at the Zen life like a kind of marathon race. You have to run real hard for a real long time but once you cross the finish line, you're done. You win. You can sit back and sip lemonade for the rest of your life. It really isn't like that at all. If anything, the opposite is true. Once you've solved those philosophical problems it's your duty to put those solutions into effect. It doesn't get easier, it gets harder.

The good news is that one of the biggest philosophical problems you clear up is the confused belief that being lazy is somehow better than working hard. Being saddled with the whole universe to take care of is better than winning the lottery or having Miss November or Mister Universe knock on your bedroom door one morning and flash you their goods when you open it. Solving those philosophical problems *does* mean you've won—but nothing so piddling as the marathon race of life. You've won all creation. It's yours to do with as you please—and you discover what pleases you most is doing the right thing for all creation in moment after moment.

As I've said, talking about enlightenment is risky—and leaving it to people's imaginations is equally risky. So nonetheless, leaving the *e*-word aside, I'll tell you about my own experience of solving the philosophical problems.

I GUESS IT WAS EARLY FALL, maybe five years after my encounter with Farting Man. I was walking to work alongside the Sengawa River, just like I did every day, when in an instant everything changed. In old Buddhist stories there's always some catalyst, like that guy who heard the pebble strike the piece of bamboo, or else someone reading a certain verse, or getting whacked by some teacher's stick. But I really can't recall anything unusual. I was just walking to work.

About a week earlier I'd finished yet another summer zazen retreat, so my brain was maybe a bit quieter than usual. Although I can't recall what I was thinking about at the time, I'm sure I *was* thinking, and probably about what I needed to do at the office that day or some similarly banal thing. I wasn't worrying or mulling over anything very deeply—just the usual stream of images bouncing around up in my head.

What I do recall very clearly is the geographical spot where it started to happen. There's a narrow road along the Sengawa River and in order to get to where I work I need to cross the river on one of the many small bridges built over it. The shortcut I like to take has me crossing one particular little bridge every morning. I was walking along the road and just about to cross that bridge when all my problems, all my complaints, all my confusions and misunderstandings just kind of untwisted themselves from each other and went *plop* on the ground. I'm not talking some of my problems, I'm talking about *all* of them, every last one. *Plop!*

Every damned thing I'd ever read in the Buddhist sutras was confirmed in a single instant. The universe was me and I was it. I looked up at the sky and that experience was exactly like looking at a mirror. I don't mean that metaphorically either. You know the feeling of recognition you get when you look in a mirror? "That's me," you think to yourself, "My hair needs to be combed and, hey, there's a pimple on my nose!" Well I got that same feeling no matter where I looked. I looked at the asphalt road and it was my face. I looked at the bridge and the bridge was me staring back at myself. It was a physical sensation, as if the sky had my eyes and could see me staring up at it. There was no doubt that this state was "true." It was far more true than the state I had considered to be normal up until then. I had no need to confirm it with anyone.

It's all me.

Even if I want to put this realization down I can't. Sometimes it's excruciating. You know those morons that rammed those planes into the World Trade Center? That was me. The people that died in the collapse. Me again. Every single person who ever paid money for a Pet Rock? Me. I don't mean I identify with them or sympathize with them. I mean I *am* them. It's impossible to explain any more clearly than that, but this isn't a figure of speech or bad poetry. I mean it absolutely literally.

But the universe is *sooooo* much bigger than any of that.

The sky is me, and the stars too, and the chirping crickets and the songs they make; sparkling rivers, snow and rain, distant solar systems and whatever beings may live there: it's all me. And it's you, too.

Was this the same state that Gautama Buddha experienced that early December morning 2,500 years ago? Yes it was. It is. Absolutely.

Is there anything special about me? Not a damned thing.

Has it changed my life? Yup.

Was it a big deal? Buddy, everything's a big deal, but yes, this was a big deal.

I'd been driving through a dark tunnel for countless years when all at once I emerged into the sunlight along the shore of a lush tropical island. Yet there were no bells, no whistles, no gongs; no thunder, no earthquakes; no peals of laughter, no tears, no drama.

And then I went to work and did my job.

It was all very ordinary and normal. But in that very normality and ordinariness was something more wonderful
than anything special I could ever have imagined. All imagination pales into nothing compared to what your real life
is right here and right now. There's not a single dream you
can have, no matter how pure or beautiful, that's better
than what you're living through right now no matter how
lousy you think right now is.

WHY SHOULD YOU BELIEVE in any of this? Why should you care?
No reason. No reason at all.

There's nothing I can possibly tell you that could communicate this state to you. Because human language by its
very nature just isn't up to the task. If I say "kumquat" or
"droopy granny boobs" or "Johnny Ramone on stage at
CBGB's circa 1975," you have an idea what I mean. But
there's nothing I can say that can communicate the reality
of that experience.

Do a lot of zazen though and you'll see it for yourself. I
can promise that, without doubt and without reservation.

But what happened to me won't happen to you. At all.
And yet it will. Exactly.

Sounds like nonsense doesn't it? I empathize.

Here's as clear as I can be about this stuff: The only
enlightenment that really matters is right here and right
now. You have it right in the palm of your hand. It shines
from your eyes and illuminates everything you see.

Oh, and one last thing: People imagine enlightenment will
make them incredibly powerful. And it does. It makes you
the most powerful being in all the universe—but usually no
one else notices.

WHY GENE SIMMONS IS NOT A ZEN MASTER

Doing zazen, you become king
of the world.
GUDO NISHIJIMA

I'm the king of the night time world!
GENE SIMMONS

WHEN I HEARD THAT KISS® was coming to Tokyo for what they were billing as their final tour (again), I had to be there. KISS® was one of my favorite bands when I was in junior high. They were the closest thing our generation had to The Beatles. I kept following them even after they committed the cardinal music sin of *going disco*. Soon after that, though, I discovered The Ramones, The Sex Pistols, The Misfits, and other bands who had the power and visual style of KISS®, but whose lyrics spoke more to my state of mind than songs about getting laid.

But now I was a grown-up and here was a chance to actually meet one of my childhood idols. The Godzilla's-feet boots that he wore in the late '70s were ample proof Gene Simmons was a major fan of Japanese monster movies. I'd even seen photos of them on one of their '70s Japan tours next to a *T. rex* costume that had been built by Tsuburaya Productions for an American made-for-TV movie called *The Last Dinosaur*. I figured maybe if I invited Gene Simmons to come down to the filming of an *Ultraman* episode I might just be able to score some good P.R. points for Tsuburaya Productions while getting to fulfill a childhood fantasy.

I wrote to Gene through the KISS® website, suspecting that probably wouldn't get me far. To my utter astonishment, I walked in a couple days later to see a message on my desk saying that someone named "Jean Simons" had called for me. It turned out he wasn't so interested in seeing the *Ultraman* set but he was trying to put together a KISS® animated cartoon. He knew Tsuburaya Productions' work and thought we might be able to help out. Would I like to come by his hotel and talk about it?

It was almost as good as the first call I'd gotten from Tsuburaya Productions!

Gene was even nice enough to get us good seats at one of the sold-out shows. The meeting was set up for the following day at the Tokyo Four Seasons Hotel—only the best for KISS®. I brought along a producer who was interested in the animation project, one of his staff people, and Atsushi Saito, the younger of my two bosses at Tsuburaya's international division. The other people took seats in the hotel coffee shop while I went to the lobby and stood watch for Gene Simmons. Paul Stanley, another KISS® band-member, came by, giving me a funny glance as I sat there in the KISS® T-shirt I'd worn to help Gene recognize me. I clearly wasn't an autograph hound since I didn't even get up when he came by. Maybe I looked like a stalker.

I couldn't possibly miss Gene Simmons when he came walking through the lobby. Even if I hadn't known what he looked like without makeup ever since *Creem* magazine ran a photo of him without it in the late '70s, his demeanor was enough to set him apart from everyone else. I've heard famous people say that they can chose to attract attention or not when going out in public simply by the way they carry themselves. Well, Gene Simmons was definitely choosing to attract attention. I led him over to our table, he took a seat and asked us if we'd enjoyed the show the previous night. I said it was good. *"Good?"* he said, noticeably perturbed. He apparently needed more than that. So I added: "It was fantastic, mind-blowing, spectacular." It really was, actually, I'd just been playing it cool and trying to be businesslike the first time. He seemed satisfied by my effusion.

We showed him some samples of our animated work and told him about the company. Actually while in the coffee shop we showed him some artwork on paper, then later on went up to his room where he had a VCR and played him a tape. I pissed in Gene Simmons's toilet! There was a *Wall Street Journal* on the floor, by the way. Then he launched into a long, self-absorbed monologue detailing his ideas for the KISS® cartoon. What was surprising to me was that the story he laid out over a bottle of Perrier® and a couple of scones showed momentary flashes of real Buddhist-style insight. The cartoon story itself wasn't Buddhism by a longshot, mind you, but there were flashes here and there of something surprisingly deep.

Furthermore, the latest KISS® album had a song by Simmons called "We Are One," some lines of which came very close to stating key points of Buddhist philosophy. "Everywhere I go, every face I see, I see my own face staring back at me"—which is about how I felt after that day by the Sengawa River. I doubt very much the meaning was quite the same for him though. But still, not a lot of people can even come up with such an idea. In his autobiography Simmons says that he has no use for Eastern philosophies but in the same paragraph he also says: "Let other people go into trances and think about spirituality. I'd rather concentrate on having something to eat. The here and now." That's the Zen view right there, after all.

This guy had played bass in one of the world's loudest heavy metal bands, spitting fire and vomiting blood and generally offending every religious pundit in America, he had never done a moment of zazen in his life, and yet he came so very close to a real understanding of certain elements of the Buddhist truth.

Did this mean he was a Zen Master? No. Not by miles. From what I could see and from what he basically owns up to in his book, Gene Simmons's main focus in life is Gene Simmons. That's hardly indication he's attained any real understanding of the nonexistence of self. But I'm sure he's glimpsed it. Perhaps only when on stage performing or, possibly backstage, er...performing. But he's never really integrated those insights into his life in such a way as to make him a Zen master or its equivalent.* On the other hand, I've seen self-proclaimed "Buddhist Masters" guilty of the very same thing who in fact had far less capacity than Gene Simmons for real honesty. But while his philosophy has many points of genuine value (and lotsa points of genuine self-gratification), I'm not quite ready to "transmit the Dharma" to Gene Simmons and declare him a Zen master.

ANOTHER ARTIST I've met who struck me as having attained a certain degree of Buddhist-type wisdom was Alex Cox, director of the films *Repo Man*, *Sid and Nancy*, and *Walker*. *Repo Man* is one of my all-time favorite movies. It's the only fictional film I know of that makes any attempt to present the early '80s American punk scene as it really was. While the rest of the media was busy making trash like *The Class of 1984* where the punks take over a school, or episodes of TV cop shows like *CHiPs* and *Quincy* in which violent "punkers" cause mayhem and murder, director Alex Cox put together a gritty, funny, and realistic film about real punk. I've lost count of how many times I've seen the film. But no matter how often I watch it, it's still

---

*Although Gene, if you're reading this, I'd like to say that CARNIVAL OF SOULS was a brilliant album that never got the credit it deserved. And thank you for the copy of KISSTORY II you sent me.

good. I've seen most of Cox's other work and have enjoyed all of it, but *Repo Man* is like *Casablanca* or *Citizen Kane*—a true cinematic classic.

When I found out Alex Cox was coming to Tokyo as part of a BBC documentary on Godzilla, I made sure to weasel my way into meeting him as well. The BBC had contacted me through a British animator friend of mine in an effort to track down some of the staff who made the original Godzilla films. I'd put them in touch with several key people, so when I begged them to let me meet Alex Cox, who was acting as the program's host, they were happy to oblige. Cox, as it happens, also loves bad Japanese monster movies. While many "serious" filmmakers turn up their noses at flicks about radioactive dinosaurs trashing Tokyo, Cox has a rare appreciation for their art.

Cox is a totally different kind of artist than Gene Simmons: he was clearly aware of the world around him. When he and I got stuck in a van together for about two hours waiting for the BBC guys to finish another interview, we talked a lot. As dopey as I must have sounded to him, he listened with a kind of intensity that was truly inspiring. There's a photo someone took of us talking, and from the expression on Cox's face, you'd think I was saying the most fascinating things in the world (I'm fairly confident I wasn't). The only other people I've met who could listen to what someone was saying with that kind of thoroughness of concentration were all Zen masters. It's possible Cox had some training in that area that I don't know about, but it's probably more to do with the nature of his relation to his art. A good film director has to pay close attention to what things look like, how people talk, how things are, if he wants to be able to translate that into a believable piece of work on screen. And Cox was just bringing this into his life.

IN OUR CULTURE TODAY celebrities mean a whole lot more than religious leaders. Most people would much rather have an audience with somebody like Gene Simmons or Alex Cox than with any religious leader of similar stature, say the Archbishop of Chicago. Vast tracts of society are far more likely to be influenced by what movie stars say than by the opinions of great theological thinkers.

Anyone who really pursues any activity to the point of becoming so good at it that millions of people want to come watch really must have understood something fundamentally real, fundamentally true. They must have understood the philosophy of action through action itself. The average religious leader, on the other hand, spends most of his time thinking about stuff. Thinking about stuff is useful, but life is more than thought.

Before I got deeply into zazen practice, I'd often noticed something different when I was working very intensively on a musical endeavor, either performing or recording. A special kind of concentration was required. When I was in that kind of concentration I'd begin to feel a kind of vast space open up—as if the room had suddenly become very open, the air itself very clear.

I used to come off the stage or out of the studio with a kind of a buzz. It wasn't like being drunk or on drugs though. It was far better. I could still function as well as, in fact *better than,* I could at other times. There was a kind of purity to the situation.

But the level of a person's celebrity status has no bearing on how truly balanced they are in their lives. Yet pretty much all of the world's famous people are famous because they have pursued some kind of artistic or athletic endeavor to the point where when they do their thing, they exhibit some truly remarkable signs of the balanced state revered in Buddhism. Our celebrities are not Zen masters but nearly all of these performers, at least when they're performing, surpass the level of balance achieved by the average person—though you have to keep in mind that the average in this case is not so high.

We may not realize it, but I suspect we care so much about what famous people say or do because we understand that their ability to focus gives them a kind of rare insight we rightly admire. We see their balance but don't see that it comes from pursuing one thing wholeheartedly. We imagine that their balance or insight comes from some inherent quality they have and we don't. Celebrities themselves are rarely any brighter than anyone else and tend to see the situation in the same mistaken way.

This kind of balance is not limited to famous people alone. It's not something that comes from having a lot of money or getting a lot of adoration or running really fast or singing really well. People with far less money or fame or "talent" exhibit signs of balance far beyond our pop-cultural heroes.

Famous people are an interesting case to observe though. Of course many of them are driven by massive ego and colossal insecurity, but there's also something more.

As I've said, Buddhist philosophy does not accept the existence of individual human beings in the way we usually conceive of them. The prevailing view of individual human beings as discrete units each acting with absolute autonomy is incomplete. It's a view that takes into account only one tiny part of the big picture and assumes that this is the whole deal.

I think in most cases most people conceive of themselves and of other people like I've illustrated in Figure I on the next page. We think of each individual as a unit with clear boundaries. Each of these units, we believe, is able to act in at least some cases with complete autonomy irrespective of the others. We consider this so obvious as to be beyond questioning.

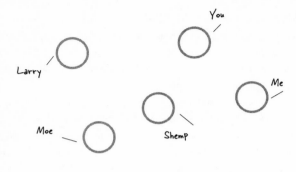

Figure 1

Our seemingly impeccable logic goes something like this: If I stand in front of you, it is very clear that my body extends only to a certain point beyond which yours begins, and there's a space between us. The space may be large or small, depending on how friendly we are and how much you resemble Maki Goto, late of the Japanese girl band Morning Musumé—but it's definitely there. You have your own thoughts which I cannot read and your own credit card which I cannot use.

We take it for granted that our perceptions are accurate and our interpretations true. We believe very strongly, literally beyond doubt, in these personal boundaries. Religions tell us that these boundaries remain intact forever and may tell us that even God too has specific boundaries.

But I don't think this way of conceiving of ourselves and others is very realistic. It leaves too many things out of the picture. I think a far better (though still necessarily incomplete) way of looking at it is as I have illustrated in Figure 2.

Reality is kind of like a sea that has waves on top of it. These small, temporary disturbances on the "surface" of reality are what we call people and things, and we conceive of them as having some kind of permanent substance or enduring individuality. We draw boundaries, rather arbitrarily, and say that the stuff within these boundaries is "me" or "you" or "that guy who used to be in The Eagles." But the waves can't really be separated from the ocean of which they are a part. In this way we can say that even our minds are made of the same stuff as everything else we encounter.

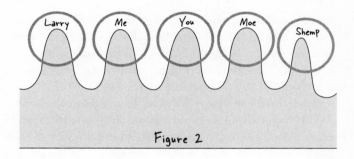

Figure 2

Celebrities don't become famous just because of the size of their chest or the force of their personality. The entire society creates the celebrity.

In fact we are all as much the creation of those around us as we are independent beings in our own right. The neat thing about famous people is that a lot of them seem to have a vague understanding of this fact. Most of them make the mistake, however, of believing it's something unique to them in particular or at least something unique to celebrities in general.

Nishijima likes to say, "When you establish the balanced state, you become the king of the world." Most of us think you need to be a celebrity for that to happen. While celebrities can do pretty much whatever they want because of their social status and their money, the rest of us feel oppressed, repressed, put upon. Gene Simmons may be king of the (nighttime) world, but you and I certainly are not.

And yet in another sense, no matter how wealthy celebrities are or how much power they seem to have, we are all absolutely equal. The only difference is that some people understand this and others do not. The entire universe is created by us and we rule over it unopposed—but for the opposition of our own minds.

The trick is we've also created certain conditions that we have to obey. In Buddhism these conditions are traditionally called the rule of the universe (or sometimes the law of cause and effect). To follow the rule of the universe is to act in a truly moral fashion. When you realize that morals are rules you have willingly imposed *upon yourself*, it's easy and natural to act in a moral way.

Because they are able to focus on doing a particular activity, artists of all kinds as well as athletes, scientists, and some others can come to understand much more of the fundamental truth of life than the average guy on the street. The problem is that while they are able to feel the balanced state of the universe when pursuing their art, they usually fail to notice it at other times. The very thing that is the source of their mental and physical balance becomes a hindrance: they begin to believe that balance is something that only occurs when scoring a basket, acting a demanding role, or strapping on a guitar and whaling away.

Lots of Zen students also fall into this trap by the way: they think that balance occurs only when they're "deeply" in zazen and at no other time. Students like this often spend far too much time doing zazen and the practice ultimately leads them further and further from true balance.

The difference between the balance achieved by a pro tennis player or a really hot drummer and that attained by a Zen practitioner is that the balance the latter have cultivated through zazen is more universal, more all-embracing. Zen people have an easier time retaining the balanced state of body and mind after getting up off the cushion than performers do after they walk offstage. Zen people also tend to have less money and be less famous, which helps— when you can get everything you think you want, you tend to spend more time and energy on fulfilling those made-up needs rather than looking honestly and critically at yourself, discovering who you truly are and what you really need. Guitar-playing or painting or what-have-you embraces just one small part of the universe. Zazen embraces everything.

THE WORLD OF DEMONS

I think of demons.
ROKY ERICKSON
FROM THE ALBUM "THE EVIL ONE"

A nightmare of shattered shapes and bizarre sensations followed by a waking nightmare of inescapable panic, a cold sweat, a racing heart. Sheer black terror. No way out.

Where am I? What's this big room? Why are there bodies all around me? Why am I on the floor?

Breathe. Think. Look. What is this place?

A temple. Ah yes, I'm in a temple!

It's a Buddhist temple, I recite it to myself. A Buddhist temple in Shizuoka. The people around me are not dead, I realize, just sleeping. It is the first night of the 1997 summer zazen retreat. There is nothing anywhere near me that could do me the least harm.

Then why am I so afraid? I want to run as far and as fast as possible, to scream bloody murder and cry for help. But where would I run to? Away from what—some nerdy-ass Zen students sleeping on the floor? I tell myself again and again there's no need for panic, there's nothing to be afraid of. Stay calm.

I tiptoe out of the sleeping room, slide open the ancient wooden door to the main hall of the temple and quietly go in. At least there are lights on out here.

I am in surroundings of utter serenity devoting my days to the pursuit of inner peace through the silent practice of zazen—what could possibly be less frightening? Still my breath comes in panting gasps, my T-shirt is soaked through with sweat and I can't stop shivering. I have never felt such panic in my life. If I'd been being pursued through a darkened alleyway by a vicious gang out for blood and armed with motorcycle chains I couldn't have felt more fear. All the fear I'd ever felt in my life has descended upon me in the middle of this night.

I sit on a bench facing the Buddha statue in the center of the main hall, a few feet from the spot where Nishijima lectured to us just hours earlier. I work hard to try to hold my body still against the shivering. I force my breathing into a normal pattern by very deliberately breathing in for a count of three, out for a count of three. I try to come up with anything real that is even potentially dangerous around here. I try hard, but can't think of anything genuinely scary. Am I having some kind of premonition of imminent danger from some unimagined source?

Gradually, I force my thought processes to return to normal through logic alone, since my emotions are completely out of control.

I realize I've had a dream and that it was some kind of subconscious message. Something in my life is causing me tremendous distress and I haven't even been aware of it. As surreal as the images are, there is a message in them that I can interpret consciously. I can see what needs to be done and I resolve to do it. I realize clearly that I am the cause of my own distress and I am the only one who can put an end to it. When my heart-rate settles and I begin to breathe normally again, I slide back into the sleeping room and crawl into my futon. After an hour or so, my mind settles enough that I fall into a troubled half-sleep.

I F YOU PRACTICE ZAZEN SINCERELY, eventually you'll encounter demons. The demons are psychological, but they're just as scary as the fiery denizens of hell. Practicing zazen is like taking the lid off a pot of boiling five-alarm chili and turning up the heat at the same time. All the stuff inside your mind wells up and spills over the edges. It can get messy.

All day long, every single day, you repress all kinds of thoughts and urges that appear in your mind. You have to—that's part of being a functioning member of society. All of us have nasty antisocial tendencies. Every last one of us. It ain't just the Nazis, al-Qaeda, and people on the registry of sex offenders—or whatever enemy-of-the-week the media is pushing. All those evil-doers are you. And me too. They're every single human being in the world without exception. Maybe you don't have whatever specific urges the media is telling you are the very worst (you tell yourself you don't, anyway), but you have others and they're just as nasty and disgusting. Every human being does. That's part of the nature of being human.

Society conditions us to ignore certain aspects of universal human nature because these aspects go against the preservation of society. All human beings have unsavory desires—but you can't have a functioning society if people are running around continually raping kittens, knifing retail clerks, and stealing old ladies' underpants. And raping, killing, and stealing are just the tip of the iceberg. There are billions of lesser urges we all have which are equally if more subtly antisocial—and those need to be repressed too. Only we don't call most of this stuff merely unacceptable or even merely antisocial. We have a much more powerful category for it. We call it "wrong" or "sinful" or "evil." What's anti-society is "wrong" and what's pro-society is "right." *True* right and wrong don't necessarily overlap completely with society's definitions of right and wrong—and different societies don't even agree on those definitions in the first place!

A lot of religious teachings sprang from the genuine understanding of certain fundamental things that had to be done or to be avoided in order to preserve society. The

Jewish prohibition against eating pork probably appeared after people had died from eating spoiled pig meat. In those days simply making the connection between such a death and the meat that was eaten was a significant leap of intelligence. But then people went on to unnecessarily conclude that this indicated that eating pork must therefore be a against God's will.

All of our religious and social codes came down to us from human beings who made connections between certain actions and their results. Sometimes their deductions were correct and sometimes they were dead wrong. But correct or not, they were passed down from generation to generation, each time gathering more psychological and social weight. Thousands of years later, one man's supposition about the connection between something he did last Thursday and some good luck he had the following weekend has become a Rule of God that none shall violate lest he be damned for eternity.

Whatever society you were born into has hundreds upon thousands upon millions of these rules, little and big. Some are so subtle you'd never even notice them. They're assumptions built into the very fabric of our languages. It's more acceptable to say "use the toilet" than "take a shit" because the former implies that you understand that good members of society take their shits in a special place called the toilet. Most words we consider obscene refer to things society wishes to ignore or at least keep very private. You go through your whole life automatically repressing those things society has taught you are "bad"—either deliberately or inadvertently. (Then of course, there are more subtle issues like the fact that most languages oblige you to reinforce the concept of *self* in every sentence: *I* am pissed. *I* like chocolate-covered slugs. *I* got enlightened.)

Most of this stuff is repressed so quickly and efficiently

that it doesn't even have time to enter into your conscious mind as a thought or idea.

You can't poop on the floor. You can't pick your nose in front of the babysitter. You can't play with your wee-wee in front of anyone. And you sure as hell can't play with someone else's wee-wee. All of this stuff gets categorized as "wrong."

Why?

There are traumas we've all carried around in our heads since before we were three years old. This deep, deep stuff is so abstract it's almost impossible to really recognize it for what it is. Think about it. The traumas you suffered as a toddler were experienced by an entity very little like what you call your "self" today. Were these things to suddenly start to flood back into your consciousness, there's no telling how your brain would end up interpreting them.

In my case, all this stuff and tons more came back up as deep, sourceless, desperate fear. Later on, the same kind of stuff popped back up as astounding dreams of fabulous wonders (more on that later).

The restrictions we place upon ourselves are the price we pay for having a civilization. There is no other way for civilization to exist. Yet we've reached a point in our own society where we can start to understand this phenomenon for what it is. Far from being the dangerous loosening of morals so many warn us about, this kind of thing is actually human society's awakening to a new sense of *real* morality, a morality that is much more powerful than any which could be maintained through the fear of a God whose existence most of us question.

WHEN YOU DO ZAZEN, you are sitting in a state in which the mechanisms of psychological repression begin to become a little more fluid, a little less restrained. That's when the demons are released from the caves we keep them in. Some people may find their repressed thoughts so alien that they take on abstract shapes or appear in the form of hallucinations, things literally experienced as "out there."

One time I actually heard the song "Kashmir" by Led Zeppelin playing all the way through, just as if there were a radio next to me. I even looked around to see if someone had brought one into the room. The demons represented in ancient paintings or spoken of in legends are nothing more than stuff just like this. Those beautiful drawings in Tibetan Buddhist art are representations of all the things that distract a person from finding the truth. The problem is that so many folks get confused and think these kinds of depictions are of the truth itself.

On the final night of forty-nine days of zazen that led to his enlightenment, Gautama Buddha is said to have faced Mara, the king of the demons. When Mara confronted him with all sorts of horrors (and all sorts of delights), Buddha touched the ground as a symbolic gesture of grounding himself in reality. You often see him in this pose in statues, sitting in the lotus position with one hand touching the ground. The story is remarkably similar to that of Christ's "last temptation" in the desert. Both stories are undoubtedly referring to the same psychological phenomenon.

Zen Buddhism speaks of *makyo* or "the world of demons." Of course there really isn't any actual realm that is the world of demons. But disturbing psychological states can seem so real that people react to them just as if they were absolutely real, and that is a problem.

Encounters with gods and demons, visits to heavenly realms and hellish ones—this stuff is fun to read about but not so relevant to people in modern Western society. These days people don't see demons and gods as much as they used to. What the ancients called visions of gods and demons and visits to heavens or hells are what we now call hallucinations, manic states, depressive states—even psychosis.

Gods and demons are culturally bound. The Salem witch-hunts, it's been theorized, were the result of several people becoming poisoned with ergot, a fungus containing the same chemical that was later synthesized and called LSD. These people believed their "visions" were the results of witchcraft. Innocent women were tortured and killed because these people did not have the understanding that certain chemicals can cause changes in the brain that can lead to the release of repressed psychological drives and can even lead to hallucinations. This is dangerous stuff.

Visions and auditory hallucinations, whether you're seeing four-armed buddhas doing the Hippy Hippy Shake or hearing talking wallabees tell you to buy an AK-47 and wipe out the office are signs of faulty processes within the brain. Nothing more. I've never exactly understood why, for example, people who hear disembodied voices seem to be inclined to do what those voices tell them. If some stranger sat down beside you on a bus and said you should break into the White House and fondle the president's dog, would you do it? Would you even consider it? Why are disembodied voices any more trustworthy? If a disembodied voice ever told me something like that, I'd tell him to go find a body and go screw himself.

Apart from my "Kashmir" moment, I've never actually hallucinated as a result of zazen. Most people these days don't. What's more likely to happen to you if you're fairly stable is that all the junk you've suppressed all your life will start bubbling up to the surface in a far subtler way.

All that suppressed stuff has gotten reshaped, twisted, and remolded by conscious and unconscious processes for decades. And what's worse is that you've given the name "me" to the result of twisting all this crap around in your brain all these years. You have to recognize that that "me" includes a lot of things that you find really disgusting and awful. You can't be truly balanced until you come to terms with this. Most people are able to successfully repress the really awful stuff at least to the point where they won't actually act it out, but pretending you don't have such urges doesn't really resolve anything on its root level. It's just denial of reality.

And neither zazen nor Buddhism is about denying reality; they're about seeing it clearly.

Recognizing your suppressed desires certainly does not mean you have to act on them. But you have to know that they're there. Pretending only abnormal people have certain desires is extremely unhealthy and extremely dangerous.

Here's why: A person discovers he has a desire that society likes to pretend exists only in truly sick and demented people. He comes to believe this desire is unique to him or at least to a very select and special group of people to which he belongs. He has every reason to believe this because society as a whole, made up as it is of people who cannot face up to the very existence of their own worst desires, tells him over and over again that this is the case. Our unbalanced friend begins to think that he *must* act upon this unique desire in order to express his own unique, "true" self. We all believe the urges that appear in our minds are somehow our "true" personality, our "real" self, and must therefore be satisfied in order for us to be really happy. Our crazy friend remains blissfully unaware, as society remains steadfastly in denial, that such desires are anything but unique. They are a universal.

Every one of us is Charles Manson, Saddam Hussein, and Adolf Hitler.

When your antisocial urges come to the surface you can feel, as I did, that it's evidence you're not a good person. You think you're just pretending to be good, fooling everyone when really you have all these terrible urges. Since the terrible urges are part of your mind, you think they must be part of "you," that they are in fact "the real you" and that the nice, normal "you" society knows is just a farce. But that's really, really not it. At all. Everyone everywhere has urges like you do. The best among us are those who see this the most clearly. You can only do good when you know what bad really is and where it comes from.

The biggest, ugliest, most damaging lie that religions spread is that truly moral people never have immoral thoughts. What a dangerous, damaging load of crap. It's not that a "good person" has only moral thoughts. It's that they act only upon the moral thoughts and not the immoral ones. Lust in your heart is not the same as adultery. Only adultery is adultery. Lust in your heart is something no one can ever, ever avoid. People who pretend they have no impure thoughts are seeking to get fat on the guilt of others.

Your desires are not what you really are. Not even close.

Your thoughts aren't the real you either. They're just electrical energy bouncing around in your brain. If you do lots of zazen you often end up going for longer and longer periods where very few thoughts occur. The brain goes quiet and Descartes' old axiom "I think therefore I am" makes no sense anymore because you're not thinking, yet *existence* still is. (But be patient with this: most folks have to do zazen many years before anything like this happens.)

What is existence *then*? Sit zazen and see for yourself.

Your opinions and preferences are not you either. A famous Zen poem called *Trust in Mind* begins, "It's easy to follow the Buddhist Way, just avoid picking and choosing." Opinions, preferences, and other such mental crap are just thoughts that have been reinforced so often they've become unconscious and nearly unavoidable habits.

Your personality isn't you either. It's just a collection of very deeply embedded opinions and preferences. Again, if you do enough zazen there will come times when even your personality ceases to function—at least in the old familiar way. Things you'd taken for granted as unique to you are seen as facets common throughout the universe.

I've said it before but it bears repeating: Everyone has a self-image, an ego. You have one, I have one, Nishijima has one, Dogen, Nagarjuna, and Gautama Buddha had one too. The difference is the way a Buddhist views his or her self-image. When a person who understands Buddhism uses the word *I*, the word is just a convenient way of locating something. The word *I* is used by Buddhists in the same way people use any other designating phase, the phrase *Les Paul guitar* for instance. You don't have any really strong attachment to the guitar (well, if it's a Les Paul, you may—but that's not what I'm talking about); you know it's just a bunch of wood held together with screws, and that the wood had its origins as parts of trees, and that the tuning keys, frets, and screws were once parts of rocks in the ground. The guitar will come apart eventually (and it'll come apart really quick if you take to a hardcore gig at a redneck bar in Ohio). But none of its components will ever really disappear. They just change form. And though they don't disappear, there comes a time when they can no longer be called a guitar. After this point you can never reassemble that Les Paul guitar no matter how hard you try. The thing that the word *I* refers to is just like that.

It's very difficult to reach this kind of understanding when it comes to your sense of self. We've been taught implicitly since birth that our "self" is something fundamental and important and real. But our self-image is nothing other than the sum total of those particular things about universal human nature we've chosen to emphasize in our own lives. Some teachings like to differentiate between "self" spelled with a little *s* and "Self" with a big *S*, but this just obscures the problem with unnecessary complications. No matter how you spell it, self is an illusion.

IF YOUR ZAZEN PRACTICE IS REASONABLE, if you're not doing too much or striving too hard to reach some goal, your demons are unlikely to appear in the form of hallucinations or massive attacks of fear and panic. But mark my words: your demons *will* appear. To experience such phenomena is a sign that your practice is maturing. The key is to not get sucked into it and to not push it away. Don't get frightened by the scary experiences and don't get seduced by the seductive ones. Keep your head. Finding a real teacher will help.

The fear I felt that night in the temple was the fear of knowing myself and the fear of what I was about to discover—that there was no me. Self is an illusion. The doctrine of no-self is such common currency in Buddhist circles that pretty much everyone who's read a few books with "Buddha" or "Zen" in the title figures they have it down pat. I did too, before that night. But I only understood it intellectually—and that was nothing like staring that truth right in the face.

Society tells you that you must suppress your urges for the good of society. Yet all of these same social codes are based upon a profound misunderstanding of who we truly are. They're based on the concept of the individual self. The concept of self relies upon past and future. "*I* have a past. "*I* have a future." You say "*I* was made fun of as a child because of my horribly out-of-fashion shoes," or fear that "*I* will die some day in a freak accident with a bowling pin." Where is that *I* who will die? For that matter, where is the *I* that is reading this word right now?

Try to define it. Try to find it. Really, really try. It's essential you do.

I lived in Africa as a child, played bass for Zero Defex from 1982 to 1984, moved to Japan in 1993, got married in 1999, and so on, and so on, and so on. Though I did all of these things, there was, from the beginning, no "self" involved in any of these actions. We tend to think of time as a line stretching from the past, to the present, and into the future, and we can see the action of cause and effect. For instance, when I was a little kid living in Nairobi, Kenya, I kept three-horned Jackson's chameleons as pets (amazing creatures they were too, just like miniature triceratopses), and these lizards left scratches on my hands that turned into tiny scars I can still see. So there is some relationship between the boy of ten in 1974 and the person who's typing this now. This is a fact, and based on these kinds of facts, we've created the idea of "self."

But time isn't really like a line.

Sure, you can find evidence that things happened, photographs, old letters, scars on your hands. But the time itself is gone. I can plan for the future. I'm writing these words right now hoping someday they'll end up in being read by someone who's interested in them. But that doesn't exist where I am now. It's a dream for me. The only thing that exists right now is the action of typing. The only real time is now. Real time is so short you can't even perceive it. Perceptions necessarily lag after the real events that trigger them. Thoughts are even further behind.

There's no past and no future. And if there is no past and no future, the concept of "self" ceases to make any sense.

It's like when The Who were on *The Russell Harty Show* in 1973. Pete Townshend pushed over one of his Marshall stack amps which fell with a thud and a crash of cymbals onto Keith Moon's drums, which in turn collapsed upon John Entwistle's Ampeg amp stacks, which also crashed to the studio floor. "Now" is like Keith Moon's drums. "The past" is Pete Townshend's amp, which created the motion by which Keith's drums now fall. "The future" is John Entwistle's amplifiers. "Self" only exists as a collective name for that series of smashes, crashes, and bangs. That's all.

"He pissed me off," we may say. The actual fact is that some action took place in the past that wasn't to your liking at some specific time. What arose in response to that action were your long-developed habits of feeling aversion to that kind of action. A "you" appeared *because* of what happened. "He pissed me off" isn't what happened. What you should say is, "being pissed off caused me to exist." "You" didn't exist until there was something for "you" to exist in relationship to, and in this case that something is something to be angry about. "You" are the reaction called "being pissed off." "You" is that sustained stream of thoughts that reinforces anger, that sees itself as being the same entity to which "he" did something in the past. It is a memory being played over and over like an old school dance-beat on a DJ's tape loop, working hard at sustaining itself, knowing that the moment it stops repeating itself "you" will cease to exist. "I'm angry" is wrong. "Right now I am anger," is closer to the truth of the matter.

My sister's ex-husband wrote me an email as he was going through the divorce proceedings with my sister, and stated our usual concept of anger wonderfully: "It's impossible not to feel angry when you are facing the gale-force winds of your emotions whipping across your body." Most of us experience most of our emotions like that most of the time.

But try this on: Experiencing anger is like sitting in the bathtub frantically thrashing around and throwing handfuls of water into the air while simultaneously wondering why the hell your head and face keep getting wet. You're in a stupor so deep you cannot even see that you're the one causing the problem. If anyone should know about this it's me, by the way. I used to like to bust things up when I got mad. A lot of my stuff still bears scars from such outbursts long ago.

It takes far more energy to sustain anger than to let it go. It only seems difficult to drop your anger because you have built up a habit of responding in a certain way to certain situations. Reacting to anger is an addiction, pure and simple, just like smoking Marlboros.® Objectively it takes more resources to keep smoking than to stop. Yet giving it up seems much harder than continuing because you're addicted.

But even the addiction of reacting to emotions isn't the root addiction. Ultimately, you are addicted to the idea of "you." It's intoxicating, fascinating, compelling. You think that there is something called "you" that perceives things, that thinks about things, that feels things and knows things. You think "you" are reading this book and evaluating whether it's true or worthwhile. But that's an illusion. Perception occurs. Thinking occurs. But there's no one doing that thinking, no one doing the perceiving. And there's no one reading this book (actually I do hope some people read this book, but you see my point).

Books on Buddhism always go on and on about "awareness" and "mindfulness." But these ideas are easily misunderstood. Being "mindful," to most people, means bringing "me" into the situation. *"I" am mindfully reading this book.* This is a mistake. To paraphrase a line in Dogen's *Shobogenzo,* real mindfulness includes you being mindful of the book, the book being mindful of you, you being mindful of you, and the book being mindful of the book. In real mindfulness, book and reader disappear completely, mind and body disappear completely. There is nothing to be aware of and no one to do it. Awareness pervades everything, awareness itself is people and books, and the smell of burning tar, the songs of birds, and all the rest.

The universe desires to perceive itself and to think about itself and you are born out of this desire. The universe wants to experience itself from the point of view of a tree, and so there are trees. The universe wants to feel what it's like to be a rock, and so there are rocks. The universe wants to know what it's like to be a famous Austrian body-builder *cum* film star and so there is Arnie. We don't know if rocks and trees have an idea of "self," and it doesn't matter one way or the other. But we do know human beings like you and me and Arnie believe in the existence of "self." And this belief is the root of all of our problems.

We all think that what we call "me" belongs to us alone. It doesn't. It belongs to the whole of the universe. You belong to the universe. And the universe is more you than "you" could ever hope to be.

The shrill clanging of the temple's brass wake-up bell shatters my uneasy rest a scant few hours after my encounter with my demons. I get dressed, wash my face, and stagger through the cool morning air into the zazen hall to start another day of staring at a bare brown wooden wall. Later that morning at the lecture someone asks Nishijima a question. I can't remember who asked it or even what the question was. But in his answer, Nishijima says, "Just stop drinking alcohol." I look up and see he is looking straight at me. I smile, he smiles back. I don't have a drinking problem. In fact I really hate alcohol, never drank much, and hadn't had any at all for years. But what he says penetrates right to the heart of my problem. The words themselves don't matter. It is direct communication.

The idea of a self is the most potent intoxicant of all.

Does Nishijima realize what he's said, what I've heard?

At the moment of such direct communication, it doesn't matter—both self and nonself vanish.

IN MY NEXT LIFE I WANT TO COME BACK AS A PAIR OF LUCY LIU'S PANTIES

If there's one thing I wouldn't want to be twice, zombies is both of them!
ED WOOD, JR.

QUESTIONS ABOUT REINCARNATION inevitably come up at every one of Nishijima's zazen retreats. In fact that was one of the first things that got me really cheezed off at Nishijima. Sometime during the second retreat of his I attended, several years before the attack of my demons, Nishijima made the sweeping statement that "Buddhists do not believe in reincarnation."

What?! Richard Gere says Buddhists believe in reincarnation and so does that guy from the Beastie Boys not to mention nearly everyone else. "*Of course* Buddhists believe in reincarnation, you old goat! Millions of people all over the world who call themselves Buddhists believe *very strongly* in reincarnation." I didn't actually say this. I just sort of sat there with black smoke coming out of my ears. I did that a lot in those days.

We're all scared of dying and we all want some kind of assurance that we're going to live forever. Having a kindly old man in black robes tell you you're going to be reborn after you die is pretty comforting. Plenty of old men in robes have made a good living that way. Nishijima's stock answer assures that at least half of the participants at his retreats go home extremely unhappy. "There is no life after death," he always says. "When you die, you never come back to life again."

When Nishijima says Buddhism doesn't accept reincarnation, arguments usually follow. But I've never once seen the old man back down.

It seems that for a lot of people today, Buddhism *is* the belief in reincarnation. There must be a hundred books at your local New Age book shop that give detailed explanations of how we move from life to life. Most of them cite the *Tibetan Book of the Dead,* a book accepted by many as a Buddhist scripture. You can find references to the idea of rebirth in pretty much any Buddhist sutra you choose to look at. Even Dogen's *Shobogenzo* is packed full of stories of people dying here and being reborn somewhere else, or even as some*thing* else—a fox, for instance. Clearly, then, Nishijima must be wrong. Buddhists *do* believe in reincarnation.

Whenever anyone—and it has frequently been me—points this out to Nishijima, particularly in connection with his beloved Dogen, he will say that these stories are just based on old Indian mythology. They're in there to add a little color to the piece. We were never meant to actually believe these people really, literally did die and get reborn somewhere else later. He likes to cite a chapter called "The Wholehearted Way" in the *Shobogenzo,* in which Dogen says the following about reincarnation:

> According to that non-Buddhist view, there is one spiritual intelligence existing within our body. When this body dies, however, the spirit casts off the skin and is reborn. If we learn this view as the Buddha's Dharma we are even more foolish than the person who grasps a tile or pebble thinking it to be a golden treasure.

The standard thing for me to do right here would be to to explain to you all of the ways in which the Buddhist idea of rebirth is completely different from the older Brahmanistic notion of transmigration. According to that theory of transmigration, there is a soul, an *atman*, that lives inside our bodies like a person renting an apartment. When the landlord, God, kicks the person out for making too much noise or not paying rent on time, the person moves to another building. We do not know if the soul gets its security deposit back, but I'm guessing that God pockets it and claims it was spent on cleaning and repairs. The Buddhist idea of rebirth, it is said, is a much more subtle view. There is no soul *as such*, the standard line goes on to say, but the conditions that created the body and mind you have now will continue after your death and manifest themselves as another form, perhaps another kind of sentient being, usually a human, in the future.

This idea ends up sounding like, "You do reincarnate, but you just don't have a soul." For years and years that's exactly how I took it. After reading Philip Kapleau's *The Zen of Living and Dying* in which he gives a very thorough and detailed explanation of why the Buddhist idea of rebirth is different from the usual idea of reincarnation I figured I had the whole thing down pat. Though Kapleau's ideas are well presented and logical, I think the best answer to the question of what Zen people think about reincarnation goes like this:

> A guy walks up to a Zen master and asks, "Is there life after death? The Zen Master says, "How should I know?" The guys replies indignantly, "Because you're a Zen master!" "Yes," says the Zen master, "but not a dead one."

When people ask about life after death they're assuming they accurately understand life *during life*. But do they? Do you?

This the one of the most important questions any of us can ask ourselves.

When Gautama Buddha was asked about life after death, eternal existence, the origin of the universe, whether space is finite or infinite, and other such imponderables, he said, "The question does not fit the case." Being less formal, I might phrase the same thing this way: "That's the wrong question, doofus!"

There's plenty of discussion on both sides about the matter of rebirth and reincarnation, but quoting quotes from books, even good ones, will never solve any problem—even the philosophical ones. If I just quoted Buddha and Dogen and left it at that I'd be like one of those guys with the bumper stickers that say, "THE BIBLE SAID IT, I BELIEVE IT, AND THAT SETTLES IT." I hate that kind of thing and I'll bet those bumper stickers don't do much for you either.

Nonetheless, I'm gonna give you my take on the whole reincarnation thing. But it's what you see for yourself— what you *realize* for yourself—that really counts. What I say here is just another thing written in another book.

But here it is:

Our brain likes to label things. That's its job. In our minds—and for the moment I'm using the words "mind" and "brain" to refer to the same thing—there is something we call "me." Our "me" consists of all of our memories, dreams for the future, likes and dislikes, ideas and opinions, thoughts and perceptions, and so on. We have a whole catalogue of "me" stuff like this. But "me" is also our label for something ineffable, something we cannot put into words. It's a name we have for something we really don't understand but assume is there. Fundamentally we don't understand *any* of the things we give names to. I might call you

"Buttnugget" but *Buttnugget* is just a name I have for an image in my brain that I associate with you. It doesn't mean I have any idea what the world looks like through your eyes.

In moments of balance and clarity, we can see that what we call "me" does not belong to us at all. It is the possession of the universe. It *is* the universe. Subject and object are the same. Nishijima says, "My personality extends throughout the universe." This something, this thing we sometimes call "me" and we sometimes call "everyone and everything else," is the same as the present moment. We think we have a mind of our own. We don't. We partake in a mind that includes all of creation. The present moment is eternal. It's always there. It is unborn and it cannot die. And it does not reincarnate.

Nor does it hold any beliefs or opinions, for or against anything at all.

You prefer The Pogues to The Backstreet Boys, but the universe does not. It should, of course, but it includes and embraces both of them equally. Yet you and the universe are one and the same.

If we sit behind the old railway station in Kent, Ohio, and watch the Cuyahoga River flow, ignoring the noise from the frat boys harassing the art students on Water Street, we'll see lots of bubbles on the river's surface. They float along on the river for a while then burst. The bubbles are just air and water. The water returns to the river. The air returns to the atmosphere. But that one bubble we watched will never appear again.

If we buy a candle at Spencer Gifts shaped like something naughty, light it, then use the flame to light a second even naughtier-shaped candle while simultaneously blowing out the first, is the flame on the second candle the same flame as the first or entirely different? Where is the first flame? Where was the sound of Tommy Ramone hitting the first rim shot on *Teenage Lobotomy* before you heard it?

After you heard it, where did it go?

Still, to say that when we die we return to the Great River of Being continues to miss the point. The notion of *returning* implies that right now we're separate from the Great River of Being or from God or from anything else. We aren't. That bubble was always part of the river even when it appeared as a bubble. We don't return to God, because we never left God in the first place.

Don't get too hooked on explanations, though. Explanations are never complete.

When we die, we die. We never appear again. Dead, dead, dead. Gone, gone, gone.

But in truth, we die all the time. Every moment of every day we die. Where is the person who slid out of your mother's womb greasy and purply-red and screaming like a banshee all those years ago? Are you that person? You have no memory of that day. It's a day that was over and done with a long, long time ago. Where is the person who lost* your virginity? Where is the person who woke up bleary-eyed and crabby yesterday morning? Where is the person who will fill your casket?

Our understanding of time is just plain wrong—and that misunderstanding leads us to believe that we *could* reincarnate, that we *could* live again after we die, that we *could* go to heaven, hell, or purgatory. That misunderstanding leads us to believe that it is even possible we might have a soul. But every one of these ideas is, ultimately, stupid. They really make no sense at all once we understand what time really is.

The moment you were born was you. The moment you die will be you. This moment right now is you. There is no difference between this moment and yourself. You live through a million you/moments every single second. Being and time are not two things. Dogen uses a compound to

*Or "will lose"—I don't want to presume.

express this just like our buddy Brundlefly. Dogen writes about "being/time." In Dogen's words "being/time is you and being/time is me."

Moments of you whip by so fast you can't possibly notice them, just like movies create the illusion of movement by showing you a series of still photos in rapid succession. The illusion of time is created by moments of you whizzing by so fast they make the standard film speed of twenty-four frames per second look glacial. The light from an electric bulb is caused by the current flickering through it, on and off and on and off, yet the light seems to be constant.

Real time is just this moment. That's all there is. There's no room for souls or for reincarnation because in order to have a soul, you need to have a past and in order to be reincarnated you need to have a future. But as I've been saying all along: You don't. Past and future are just ideas. When there is no past and no future, the question of life after death in any form including reincarnation becomes entirely irrelevant. This is what Gautama Buddha was talking about when he said, "The question does not fit the case."

All the problems I've ever had all stem from being unwilling to stay with the life I'm living right this moment. And the same goes for all your problems. Sort out your misunderstanding of time and all your problems go away. Just like that.

MY WIFE WORKS MOST WEEKENDS and I do not. But last week she had Sunday off. She planned a day out for us at Kunitachi, an area on the far west part of Tokyo where there's a beautiful university with spacious grounds and a lovely Chinese vegetarian restaurant. All week I was looking forward to that trip. It was pleasant knowing that I'd get to go out there and spend time with Yuka that day.

It took forever but Sunday finally came. There we were out in Kunitachi walking around, enjoying the sunshine and fresh air. We sat down on a bench on the campus, and all of sudden a bunch of college baseball players decided to change out of their uniforms and into their street clothes right next to us. I found myself distressed: Was Yuka comparing their tight jockey shorts–clad teenage buttcheeks to my flabby mid-thirties ones?

A bit later I noticed my feet were starting to get sore from all the walking. The thought occurred to me, *"I wish I were home."*

THIS HAPPENS TO ALL OF US all the time. The only special trick a Buddhist has is to avoid being sucker-punched by these thoughts when they come up—as they always will. A Buddhist learns that his thoughts are just thoughts, nothing requiring any response. But most of us feed into them: a little spark of a complaint appears and instead of letting it die out, we stoke it up. If we work really hard at it, we can make a tiny spark can turn into a raging blaze in no time at all. Then we get upset because it's getting too hot. Once the blaze has gotten that big, though, it's hard work to put it out. What's worse is that we have no idea *how* to put it out. Our efforts just end up making the flames bigger and bigger until it's completely out of control consuming every moment of our lives.

Reincarnation is all very much tied in with this. We're just trying to establish for ourselves the existence of something that has no reality. We're trying to preserve that something that makes us miss out on a beautiful day in the country by telling us we'd really be much happier back in the city, and makes us miss out on the beautiful chintziness of a Muzak® rendition of "Smells Like Teen Spirit" at the dentist's office wishing we could be at home listening to Kurt Cobain. We try so hard to preserve the very thing that's making us miserable. We cling hard to our pain because we mistakenly think that that pain is who we really are. We define ourselves by what we don't like or we define ourselves by what we like. Either way we miss the truth. We harbor some inexplicable fear that if we start to enjoy everything about life without picking and choosing we might cease to exist.

THE DENIAL OF REINCARNATION might sound like a terrible thing, a promise that nothing's waiting for you at the end of your life but bleak, black nothingness. In fact, I don't know what's waiting at the end of our lives. No one does. But it's not the future that matters. Right now is what counts. If you want to believe in reincarnation, you have to believe that *this life*, what you're living through right now, *is* the afterlife. You're missing out on the afterlife you looked forward to in your last existence by worrying about your next life. *This* is what happens after you die. Take a look.

You can get hooked on afterlife ideas just like a drug. The reason to avoid ideas about life after death isn't because they couldn't possibly be true. Maybe they could. How would I know? It's because ideas like that promote a kind of dreamy fantasy state that distracts us from seeing what our life is right now.

"The question doesn't fit the case."

Look at your life as it is right now and live it, right now.

THAT'S *ZEN MASTER* KNOW-IT-ALL to YOU, BUDDY!

I'm a cop. You will respect
my authority.
ERIC CARTMAN on SOUTH PARK

DHARMA TRANSMISSION is a very controversial subject within Zen circles. Back when Gautama Buddha was alive there was an incident in which he stepped up to give a talk. As was customary in India, flowers had been strewn at his feet before he began to teach. Instead of speaking, Gautama just picked up one of those flowers and held it silently aloft—and a guy named Mahakashyapa, one of his long-time students, smiled. Then the Buddha winked at a him, called it day's teaching, and walked away.

This little scene is viewed by Zen Buddhists as the moment when the Buddha recognized that one of his followers had attained the same level of understanding as he had himself. The Buddha's silent wink was taken to be the start of the formal acknowledgment known today as Dharma Transmission.

But 2,500 years have passed since then and a lot of things have changed. In Japan, it's not all that hard to find the head of some temple, some guy who "has transmission" who will give it to you if you can show him you've got a good reason to have it—and unfortunately having just inherited the family temple from your old man counts as a good reason. Oh, and you also have to have enough bank to pay certain associated "fees" to the head temple. Many Japanese priests today give transmission for a variety of reasons that have nothing to do with real understanding of Buddhist truths; a lot of it's simple politics, business, or nepotism.

To me, though, as for a lot of American Zen students, Dharma Transmission was always a big deal. So when Nishijima told me, very casually one day, that he wanted to give me transmission, I was taken aback. I resisted the idea. It scared me. Who the hell was I? How I could possibly "deserve" that? But Nishijima made it clear that while I could delay the actual ceremony, as far as he was concerned I had already "gotten" transmission. Still, I put it off.

I TOOK NEARLY A YEAR to decide to accept Dharma Transmission. To accept such a thing is to become an authority figure and I've always had a problem with authority. I never liked authority figures, never wanted to be an authority figure, and never gave a shit about the people who did. Never trusted 'em. In my whole life I've hardly ever come across an authority figure who really deserved the power that had been conferred upon her or him. My teachers and school administrators had by and large shown themselves to be hardly worthy of my contempt let alone my respect. Mister Walters, my junior high principal, once put me through such intense psychological torture I nearly puked all over his floor—and in retrospect I wish I had!—and then he revealed that he had no idea who I was or why I'd been called to his office. It's hard not to feel contempt after such an experience. The few people in positions of authority I did respect never played the whole Authority Figure role.

And as authority figures go, religious authority figures were definitely the worst—and now here I was about to become one. I was conflicted, to the say the least.

Of course rebellion against authority, as any pop-psychologist will tell you, is just an immature and maladjusted psychological reaction to the traumas of a childhood, when the Big Bad Adult told us we were forbidden from doing something or other we wanted to do, and learning not do everything we want all the time is part of the normal process of socialization. Every child rebels against this to some degree, but eventually, a mature person accepts some amount of authority.

Unfortunately, what happens to most people is that they don't just *accept* authority, they *believe* in it. We have, buried within us, an unspoken, unacknowledged belief that there are some people who are somehow better than others, more deserving than ourselves—that authorities are somehow *worthy* of the authority they wield.

We don't believe in divine kings anymore but we still believe in our celebrities in much the same way. Intellectually we know they're just like us. But on a deeper psychological level we regard them somehow as *special* beings, endowed with some kind of extraordinary powers lowly creatures like ourselves do not possess.

Why did so many people take notice in 1966 when John Lennon said The Beatles were bigger than Jesus? Because he was a celebrity. He was special in our eyes because he wrote good songs and so he became an Authority. Happens all the time.

I was personally shocked to discover this particular belief buried in my own psychological makeup, despite the fact that I'd spent much of my life penning sarcastic ditties about stupid people who trusted their stupid leaders and prayed to their stupid God and stupidly worshiped their stupid pop heroes.

It never occurred to me to examine my unspoken belief that *my* heroes—John Lennon, Syd Barrett, and Robyn Hitchcock—were obviously *worthy* of reverence and that therefore my unquestioned belief in them was duly called for. I also believed in Eiji Tsuburaya, special-effects man behind the Godzilla series, and subsequently in his son, Noboru who became my boss when I started working for Tsuburaya Productions. These men were obviously something apart from ordinary humanity. They were Authority.

Noboru Tsuburaya's death from cancer in 1995 brought home to me in no uncertain terms the fact that I still believed in Authority. I was truly stunned. I had erected an imaginary barrier between Him and me that prevented me from even asking if I could make a visit to His bedside. How could a lowlife like me presume to be in the hospital room of such a great man? I made up all kinds of excuses—until time finally ran out and he was gone. Not having said goodbye to him is one of the greatest regrets I have.

But my belief in Authority went even deeper than I'd suspected. Even after throwing away what I'd thought was the final vestige of my belief in Authority, I still had one category of Authority Figures left: Zen masters. Zen masters had always been above the stuff I hated in other Authority Figures. Tim and Nishijima certainly had shown themselves worthy of real respect. The ancient Zen masters I read about in books were mythical figures, towering above the rest of mankind. In short, they were Authority.

My belief in the Nishijima's authority prevented me from being able to speak honestly with him for many years. I used to wonder why he often fell silent during our conversations. I'd always break out in a cold sweat whenever that happened and try desperately to come up with something clever or insightful that might impress him. But when I did come up with some little nugget, he'd just cock his head and give me a quizzical look. So I'd end up saying a nervous goodbye and racing out of the room feeling like a real schmoe. It took far longer than it should have for me to learn that all he was waiting for was for me to speak sincerely, person to person. When I did that, conversation with him was totally natural.

NOW HERE HE WAS offering to make *me* a "Zen master." Not even offering, really, here he was saying I was already a "Zen master" and he just wanted to do a formal ceremony acknowledging that fact. To make matters even worse, not only did Nishijima want to give me Dharma Transmission, he wanted me to got through a ceremony called "receiving" the Buddhist precepts first.

The ceremony of receiving the Buddhist precepts is the closest thing you'll find in Japanese Zen Buddhism to what's called "being ordained" in most religions. Nishijima wanted me—*me!?*—to become an ordained priest in a major world religion?

Pull the other one, it's got bells on it!

NO SEX WITH CANTALOUPES

Never let your sense of morals keep you
from doing what's right.
ISAAC ASIMOV

ALTHOUGH RECEIVING THE PRECEPTS basically amounts to ordination in Japanese Zen, the precepts themselves are common to all sects of Buddhism, and receiving them essentially amounts to committing to live an ethical life. But whatever the style and whatever the dress requirements, the basics of the ceremony remain the same: the student agrees to abide by what are known as the ten fundamental precepts. These are:

1. not to kill,
2. not to steal,
3. not to misuse sexuality (or "not to desire too much" as Nishijima likes to phrase it),
4. not to lie,
5. not to cloud the mind with intoxicants,
6. not to criticize others,
7. not to be proud of yourself and slander others,
8. not to covet,
9. not to give way to anger,
10. not to slander the Three Treasures.

Number 10 is not quite as obvious as the others. Don't sweat it. Bear with me here.

THERE ARE NO MATTERS OF "SIN" in Buddhism, so unlike breaking one of the Ten Commandments, breaking one of these ten precepts is not considered sinful. In fact, there may be situations in which breaking one of the precepts is the appropriate thing to do and maintaining it literally would be "wrong."

Rather than being a set of rules that must be followed in order to avoid the Wrath of God, the ten precepts are a set of general guidelines describing ten actions that are almost always detrimental to the establishment of good relations among and within human beings. Engaging in any of these activities pretty much ensures that a certain degree of what's commonly called "bad karma" will follow. "Bad karma" is, by the way, a terrible phrase. The word *karma* just means "action." But since we cannot take any action without some kind of consequences following, the word *karma* has commonly been misunderstood as referring only to the consequences of our actions and not the actions themselves. Actions and their consequences always appear simultaneously, though our brains are stuffed so full of cotton-candy we presume they take place sequentially.

Since Gautama Buddha's time, all Buddhists have taken a vow to uphold some version of this list of precepts (some lists are longer, some shorter). But aside from these fundamental precepts, there's a huge of list of other precepts, called the *vinaya* precepts that some sects also follow.

These came about because during Gautama's lifetime, people would ask him if some particular thing—sex with cantaloupes, for instance—was right or wrong, and if he said it wasn't right, one more vinaya precept was added: "Not to have sex with cantaloupes." It went on and on like this for the over forty years Buddha taught.

Someone would ask: "Is playing the *Sonic Reducer* on electric guitar bad, O Wise One?" "Only if you play *Sonic*

Reducer so loud it annoys the neighbors," Buddha would answer rather reasonably. And this was handed down from generation to generation as precept number 1394(a): "Not to play *Sonic Reducer* on the electric guitar so loud it annoys the neighbors."

As he was dying Gautama called Ananda, his cousin and longtime assistant in administrative matters, to his side. Gautama said to him that it was important to keep the major precepts, but that the minor ones could be more or less ignored. Unfortunately the sage didn't go so far as to actually specify exactly which precepts were major and which were minor. Sometime later, though, it was agreed that the ten precepts listed above (or maybe just the first five) were the really important ones. The others have been largely relegated to the history books and certain strict sects of Theravada Buddhism.

IN ZEN, we also have another take on the ten fundamental precepts, from a guy called Bodhidharma, the Indian monk who brought Buddhism to China from India several centuries after Gautama Buddha's death. He probably actually existed, but probably didn't do or say all the things attributed to him. But as I mentioned, Buddhists really don't care one way or the other. Anyhow, Bodhidharma left us a very famous reinterpretation of the ten precepts. His versions go like this (and by the way, the word *Dharma* below means "the way things are"):

1. Self-nature is mysteriously profound. In the everlasting Dharma, not giving rise to the notion of extinction is called the precept of not taking life.
2. Self-nature is mysteriously profound. In the Dharma in which nothing can be obtained, not giving rise to the thought of obtaining is called the precept of not stealing.

3. Self-nature is mysteriously profound. In the Dharma in which there is nothing to grasp, not giving rise to attachment is called the precept of not misusing sex.

4. Self-nature is mysteriously profound. In the inexplicable Dharma, not speaking even a single word is called the precept of not telling lies.

5. Self-nature is mysteriously profound. In the intrinsically pure Dharma, not allowing the mind to become dark is called the precept of not dealing in intoxicating liquors.

6. Self-nature is mysteriously profound. In the faultless Dharma, not speaking of others' faults is called the precept of not criticizing others.

7. Self-nature is mysteriously profound. In the sphere of equal Dharma, not speaking of self and others is called the precept of not being proud of self and slandering others.

8. Self-nature is mysteriously profound. In the all-pervading true Dharma, not clinging to one form is called the precept of not coveting.

9. Self-nature is mysteriously profound. In the Dharma of no-self, not giving rise to the thought of self and others is called the precept of not giving way to anger.

10. Self-nature is mysteriously profound. In the one Dharma, not giving rise to the thought of distinction between sentient beings and Buddhas is called the precept of not speaking falsely of the Three Treasures.

Interesting, huh?

SO WHAT'S THIS SAY about Buddhist morality? There are nitwits out there who'll tell you Buddhism, particularly Zen Buddhism, isn't concerned with morality, that it's enlightenment that really counts. They're wrong. Enlightenment is for sissies. Living ethically and morally is what really matters.

Some of my best friends are people who've made it their business to try to solve all the world's ills—and God love 'em for it. Most people think this kind of behavior is the most intensely moral thing anyone could engage in. My friends certainly do.

For years and years I labored under the impression that people like this were really "doing something" while I was just sitting around staring at walls or contemplating my navel lint (it keeps coming back—what's up with that?). But is what they do what it really means to be moral? When you decide that helping feed homeless transgender crack addicts to the baby whales—or whatever—is somehow more worthy than helping your mom clean the dead squirrel out of the gutters, that's when you get in trouble. It's not that the "worthy" causes aren't worth pursuing—of course they are. It's that all too often our image of "worthy" causes completely obscures the stuff right under our noses—and *that's* the stuff that needs our attention, right here and right now.

Probe into it and you start to see that there are plenty of people who run around telling the world they're "committed" to whatever cause it is they're trying to make right but who have no commitment at all to handling their lives at this very moment or even treating the people they encounter day-to-day in a civil fashion. Back when my punk friends and I were shouting about America's ever-increasing and highly illegal incursions into El Salvador, Ronald Reagan's dangerous policy of nuclear brinksmanship, and the Moral Majority's war on the freedom of speech—what were our lives really like? We couldn't even get it together to keep the toilets running. I may have been committed to the El Salvadoran struggle, but where was my commitment to my toilet? Where was my commitment to putting decent food in my body so that my brain could think clearly enough to say something intelligent about the issues that had me so vexed? Where was my commitment to putting my Black Flag records back on the shelf and vacuuming everybody's cigarette butts off the rug? Where was my commitment to just not being an asshole?

When you're so committed to the future, it's real easy to let your life right now turn to shit.

WE'RE CONSTANTLY DRAWING imaginary distinctions between "big" issues and "little" ones. And we think only the "big" issues matter. Actually, though, the tiniest bit of good you do makes the world a better place for everyone. Cleaning those weird orange stains of unknown origin off the toilet isn't solely going to bring about lasting peace in the Middle East, but it helps. It really does. It's part of a chain of cause and effect that affects you and affects the universe. And life for everyone gets a little better. A little of that goes a long way. And it's really impossible to know exactly how or how much.

Chaos theory has it that a butterfly flapping its wings in Central Park can cause a hurricane in South America. Don't discount the similar effect of smiling genuinely at someone you don't really like all that much.

Real morality isn't just refraining from doing stuff that's outrageously heinous. Real morality encompasses every thing you do every minute of every day. It includes the way you say "good morning" at work, the way you pay your utility bills, the way you deal with the driver who cuts you off on the freeway. It includes the way you eat and sleep and breathe and scream. It includes how you dress yourself and style your hair—not that there are "moral dress codes" or "moral hairstyles," but the way you approach the thing matters. In the movie *Stardust Memories*, Woody Allen meets some aliens and starts asking them all the Big Questions About Life. They tell him, "You're asking the wrong questions. If you want to make the world a better place, tell funnier jokes!"

Do what you do as well as you possibly can. That's Buddhist morality.

Real morality comes from each individual, from each of us. Yet this isn't an "I make my own rules, man!" morality. Morality has nothing whatsoever to do with rules—not my rules, not your rules, not Buddha's rules. Real morality is based on a single criterion: right action, *appropriate* action, in the present moment and present situation. Doing what's right in this moment is the only good there is, doing what is not right at this moment is the only evil. A war stops when people stop firing guns at each other. Treaties and ceremonies are just window-dressing. World peace happens when no one fires guns at anyone anymore.

You bring about world peace when you bring about peace within your own body and mind.

Man that sounds lame! I used to laugh out loud at that kind of thing and it still looks like a load of hippy-dippy crap when I see it written down. And yet, as it turns out, it's also true. It's what I've seen, based on my own experience in my own life. And it's what you'll see if you really take the time to look.

Real morality is based on seeing how the universe actually operates and avoiding doing those things that make ourselves and others miserable. It's not that if we're "bad" when we're alive, we go to hell when we're dead. It's not that if we do wrong now, we'll have "bad karma" recorded on some kind of cosmic accounting ledger and we'll be spend our next life as a dung beetle. God is the source of you and you are the source of God. If you understand the natural law of cause and effect in your bones you naturally refrain from doing stupid things—because it all happens to you. You create the cause and you experience the effect.

There are people who think that they can do wrong and get away with it, even profit from it. It don't work that way.

This is always and inevitably the case. No one gets away with murder. No one gets away with anything. You can't escape the consequences of your immoral acts any more than someone who drops a big-ass amp directly on his foot can escape having broken toe-bones. Your life and the life of everyone else in the universe are one seamless whole. To cause another living being pain isn't evil—it's just stupid. Because that being is you.

THE INTERESTING THING is that the more clearly you understand the law of cause and effect, the faster the law appears to operate—because in actual fact, cause and effect operate simultaneously. The cause *is* the effect. For the severely deluded, things may seem to take a very long time to have any effect. That's why a successful thief thinks he's gotten away with something. He hasn't, he's just too boneheaded to see what's happening even now. The degree of your delusion determines how long it takes to notice the effects you've created.

Maybe you think you've got this down pat—you don't, by the way, because it's an ever-changing thing that can't possibly be pinned down—but maybe you think you do. But what about those other people out there? What about the people in the Middle East who seem like they never will? What about gang members on the streets of Parma, Ohio? What can you do about them?

You want peace in the Middle East? Do what Nishijima did at the spry age of eighty-two, a month after the September 11th tragedies in 2001: Go to Israel and tell people about this stuff. And if the people you talk to won't listen, go and tell somebody else. And maybe in a few decades, word will begin to spread. Or maybe it won't. Treat the people you meet with kindness and respect. Go out and appreciate the beauty of billowing smoke from a tire factory or the spectacle of sunset over the city dump. Appreciate your life and help others appreciate theirs. Stop the racist, gay-bashing Nazis from going to war to club baby seals in the burning South American rainforests if you want—but also clean your room.

The major problems we have in the world are nothing more than big ugly heaps of much smaller, much more mundane problems. But ultimately, taking care of the small takes care of the large. Of course, we do have to work out some of those really big issues before they kill us all. But even here we have to do what needs doing step by step with the flexibility to change tactics when things don't go as planned.

Do the things you can do right here and right now. Do your best. And when you run into something that you can't fix, keep on doing your best. Take things as they come one by one by one. And gradually, you'll find that things start looking a little better. But bear in mind that "gradually" will happen on the universe's time scale—not necessarily yours. Be patient. You'll never be rid of all your troubles—and really, you wouldn't want to be. The miracle is—and just think about this one for a little bit—if enough people start doing the right thing here and now then ever so gradually, ever so very agonizingly slowly, all of those big hairy world problems will just

simply

disappear.

In fact, that's already happening.

But I'll say it again: If you want to really change the problems of the world, you have to start with yourself. You have to look at your own action right here and right now. You are the only one you can ever change. Your opinions, your beliefs, your traditions, the habits you picked up from your family and your culture, they're all of no value at all when it comes to true morality. Tell funnier jokes!

You need to learn to observe yourself clearly and with a penetrating honesty that melts right through your own thoroughly built-up defenses. And trust me, this is far more difficult than it sounds.

Reality is here and now. The universe is where you are at this moment. The most important action you can possibly take is what you do right now. Be completely naked. Be absolutely open and the universe will show itself in all of its true glory. God will stand before you and within you.

REVENGE of the POD PEOPLE

I don't want to belong to any club that
will accept me as a member.
GROUCHO MARX

WHEN I WAS STUDYING ZEN with Tim McCarthy, Buddhist morality was definitely talked about but there was never any question of me or anyone receiving the Buddhist precepts from Tim. Tim just wasn't into that kind of ceremonial stuff. When I got to Japan and started studying Buddhism with Nishijima, I gradually became aware that a lot of his students were taking the precepts ceremony and that he already had a few "Dharma heirs"—people to whom he'd given transmission. I noticed that lots of people showed up at his lectures wearing a thing called a *rakusu*. This is a little garment deal that looks kind of like a bib: a square of cloth, usually brown or gray or black, that you hang around your neck. On the back of the cloth square your teacher writes a short phrase usually from a Buddhist sutra and your "Dharma name"—a new name which is given to you when you take the precepts ceremony. All of that stuff has always seemed really lame to me.

I've always held disdain for people who join spooky mystical religious orders and then change their names and start wearing goofy orange dresses and all kinds of other weird affectations. My buddy Terry of the Cleveland Hare Krishna temple is a good example of what happens to that sort of person.

But everybody loves getting a nickname. Nicknames are fun. Though it wasn't the coolest name, I was pretty pleased when the guys in Zero Defex started calling me Brad No Sweat. I would have preferred something more along the lines of the punk names my friends Johnny Phlegm and Fraser Suicyde got, but it was good enough. I rarely used that name, though, because, well, I hated the whole idea of using fake names. Taking on a fake name is a way of signaling membership in a group. And I was *not* a "joiner."

I was always disgusted whenever I saw the people in Nishijima's group proudly showing off their new rakusus. It made the whole organization look like a cult. Uniforms are things you wear when you get a job at Burger King. What's a rakusu, really, other than a fancy kind of name-tag: "Welcome to Buddhism! My name's Brainwashed Twit!" So when people in Nishijima's group used to say to me, "You ought to take the precepts," I felt like I was in one of those bad horror movies where everybody's gradually being taken over by the aliens and I am the only human being left in town—Pod People coming at me from every direction: *"Join us! Join us!"* It creeped me out.

ALL OF THIS STUFF with Nishijima wanting me to join his cult and become an Authority Figure within it happened to coincide with my grandfather being diagnosed with cancer. He was already eighty-one years old and the doctors felt that surgery at that age might kill him faster than the disease which seemed to be progressing extremely slowly. At one point he was sent to the hospital for observation and I decided I'd better go and visit him rather than wait until it was too late.

Plus, the visit would give me a chance to stop by Tim's place and talk to him about this whole Dharma Transmission deal. Tim was still in Kent which was four hours' drive from where my grandpa was, down in Cincinnati. I arranged to arrive in Cleveland, spend a few days in Kent, and then head for Cincinnati. Grandpa, my aunt and my grandmother said, was doing pretty well under the circumstances and there was no reason to hurry. When I spoke to Grandpa on the phone he sounded strong and even told me it was a waste of money to come all the way to America just to see him.

My grandmother, my aunt, and the doctors were wrong. Grandpa died suddenly just hours after I arrived in the country. I found out when the friend I'd arranged to stay with got a frantic call from my dad while I was out visiting Tim's place. Several hours later when I finally got the message, I was devastated. After that, talking to Tim about Dharma Transmission didn't seem so important anymore.

I LOVED MY GRANDFATHER DEARLY. He was a true friend and always supportive of whatever I did in my life. I'd worried about his reaction when I was telling him about my moving to Japan—because he'd joined the navy in World War II in order to fight those people. But he was fine with that and he was pleased when I brought home a Japanese wife for him to meet. It was tough to lose him.

Since I come from a long line of agnostics we had no family pastor to call on to perform the funeral. My grandmother ended up finding some random religious guy in the phone book. He seemed sincere enough—but he'd never met my grandfather. We talked with him briefly a couple hours before the funeral was set to begin and he asked the family members if they would say a few words at the service. My dad and I volunteered, hoping others would follow suit. But no one did. My dad made it through his bit very well, I thought. Knowing Grandpa's love of humor I prepared a joke as part of my speech. I said that I'd come out from Japan to visit my grandpa, not to attend his funeral. In fact, I said, Grandpa had told me in our last phone conversation that if he did die soon, I was not to waste my money coming to his funeral. But, I said, since I was already in town and had nothing else to do that morning, I thought I'd drop by.

I wasn't sure how everyone would take the joke (a funeral parlor's a tough room to work), but I got a laugh so I guess the speech went over pretty well. Afterward my grand-mother took me aside and asked, "Do you think there's any way he could know we're all here and we're all thinking of him?" Without thinking about the question I surprised myself by honestly saying, "Yes. I do. Absolutely."

I've often wondered where that answer came from. It was spontaneous. It wasn't based on any particular belief I held— in fact it went against a lot of them—but I wasn't just being kind. Grandpa *was* there in any and every sense that really mattered. Not as a ghost hanging out in the corner checking up on things, but as a real participant in the living events of that afternoon. Shunryu Suzuki once said, "You will always exist in the universe in one form or another." Even without holding any ideas about reincarnation or the afterlife or spir-its, I saw right now that Suzuki's words were true.

SOMETIME DURING MY TRIP I decided to accept Dharma Trans-mission from Nishijima and to get on with doing what needed to be done. Hell, as long as there were going to be Authority Figures in the world, I might as well be one of them. When I got back home I got in touch with Nishijima and asked him what arrangements needed to be made. He set a date, and that was that.

The precepts ceremony was fairly unremarkable, and not as bad as I had feared. Yuka decided to take the precepts too, as did a friend of ours named Eric who was stationed in Japan serving, the U.S. Navy. Nishijima got dressed up in some silly-looking official-type precept-giving robes. An altar was set up and there was some incense-lighting, some bowing, a bit of chanting, and at the end of it, all three of us got rakusus with our new Buddhist names written on the back.* Mine, as I mentioned earlier, was Odo, which means "The Way of Answers." And like my Krishna buddy Terry, it was chosen partly because it sounds a little like "Warner"—that is, if you're an eighty-two-year-old Japanese Zen master it does. By the way, Nishijima's Dharma name, Gudo, means "The Way of Stupidity." Really.

Next up was the biggie, the Dharma Transmission ceremony (imagine monster truck racing–cavernous echo here). For this, I had to get myself a *kesa*, the traditional robe worn by Buddhist monks since Gautama Buddha's time. Zen monks in Japan normally wear two main garments. One is a big black robe and over the top of this is a thing that looks kind of like a sash. It's usually mustard-colored or brown, though I've seen purple too. The sash thingy is the kesa. In India, where its considerably hotter than Japan, the kesa was the monk's only garment.

Traditionally you're supposed to sew your own kesa, and your supposed to do it from discarded scraps of cloth from burial shrouds as well as diapers and sanitary napkins. Some people still sew them themselves, but I don't think even they go so far as to use shrouds, diapers, and sanitary napkins. When I asked Nishijima for his recommendation he said, "You can sew it if you want to. I bought mine in a store." I've never even sewn a button on a shirt, so I found a shop and bought a kesa (the cotton was new, by the way).

The other thing I needed was a certificate of transmission for Nishijima to sign and stamp with his seal. This I had to make for myself.

* If you just have to know the hardcore details of the ceremony, check out a book called ZEN IS ETERNAL LIFE by Jiyu-Kennett In spite of the awful title (it used to be brilliantly titled SELLING WATER BY THE RIVER) the book is a pretty useful guide to the basic ceremonies and core texts of the Soto sect of Zen Buddhism.

I was to take a big piece of silk and write down the names of all the people who ever received the transmission in Nishijima's lineage starting from Gautama Buddha all the way through Nishijima's teacher and Nishijima himself and then adding my own name—or rather the new phony Buddhist name I'd received at the previous ceremony—at the end. Though he told me I could write the names in roman letters, I elected to write them in Chinese characters. I liked the challenge of it and besides, he showed me a photocopy of one of his other foreign student's transmission certificate and it looked dorky written in roman letters. I ruined two pieces of silk, and finally, after messing up the names of two of my Dharma ancestors, I asked Nishijima if I could use Wite-Out® to correct the mistakes rather than toss away another piece of silk. "Sure," he said without hesitation.

The details of the ceremony itself are supposed to be secret. I guess they're worried that if they get out, unlicensed people might start transmitting each other willy-nilly and then *who knows* what kind of hell would break loose. So, in fairness to everyone who's been keeping mum about it for the past dozen centuries, I won't go into the details here. But you're not missing much.

Traditionally it's supposed to take place after midnight. But Nishijima doesn't like to stay up that late, so the fun began at 8:30 in the evening. I pretty much got every single step in the ceremony completely wrong. My kesa kept sliding off my shoulder, I kept putting the little mat-thingy you're supposed to kneel down on the wrong way around, I nearly klonked heads with Nishijima when we were bowing to each other—pure comedy.

But I got through it and Nishijima gave me my certificate back with all the necessary seals on it—and, *badda bing, badda boom*, I'm a certified Zen master.

LET ME TELL YOU THIS THOUGH: No one masters Zen. Ever. It's a lifelong, never-ending continuously unfolding process. *Zen master* is a horribly misleading term.

Could we dispense with Zen masters? Certainly. Could we dispense with the Dharma Transmission ceremony altogether? Sure. And we could dispense with the word *Buddhism* too. Personally, I'd like to get rid of all of them. Ultimately, none of it has anything to do with what matters.

Gautama Buddha was able to see through the façade of religious organizations and must certainly have realized that his simple method of meditation ran a serious risk of being turned into something cheap and shoddy by association with such nonsense. In fact he predicted his own order's eventual demise. Yet he went ahead and established an order of monks, and one of nuns, anyhow. He knew it was the best way to transmit what he had found to future generations. It worked, too—for all the cheap gaudiness that surrounds much of what passes for "Buddhism" today, Buddhism works. Real Buddhism still makes it through the institutional Buddhist muck, like a flower blooming out of a cow-pie.

No matter how many dumb-asses there are running around with shaved heads and robes who wouldn't know enlightenment from a poke in the eye with a sharp stick, there are some people within Buddhism who know *exactly* what it was Gautama Buddha was trying to teach. And these people, these real Buddhist teachers, also know better than to believe in the institutional façade referred to as "Buddhism." And they know this precisely because of the social organization known as Buddhism. Neat, eh?

Any good Zen Buddhist teacher will tell you right up front that the whole Zen Buddhist shebang, from robes to enlightenment to Dharma Transmission, is really a sham, ultimately not important in the least. And *that's* what makes Zen Buddhism different from every other religion.

As Johnny Rotten said in *MOJO* magazine, "It isn't a rip-off if you tell everybody it's a rip-off." Authority is easily abused. But authority can do good. It takes power to make the real changes needed in the world. A good person who is good at dealing with power can make the world a better place for everyone.

Buddhism, though, should go beyond that. Buddhism is about letting people know they do not need to follow any authority. If you think you need an authority figure, go somewhere else.

The tendency to look at Buddhist teachers as Authorities is tough to avoid. I noticed my teachers were different from me in some vague way I couldn't really understand, and so I gave them Authority. But, God bless 'em, they always tossed it right back to me. That's what any good Buddhist teacher does. That's the easiest way to tell the real teachers from the phonies: a phony will take your authority and a real teacher will give it back.

There are times I've felt I could do certain people some good *if only* I could get them to see me as some kind of authority—but that kind of attitude isn't right. A faith-healer makes people believe he has a special power to cure their sickness and if they believe that strongly enough, they may be able to transcend their own inability to see that they themselves have the power to affect their own cure. The problem is that they then attribute their miraculous healing to the faith-healer instead of to themselves thereby depriving themselves of the power that was already theirs to begin with.

Ultimately it's always better to make people see how they can heal themselves. That's what real Buddhism does. Real Buddhist teachers don't tell you about reality, they teach you to *see* reality for yourself, right now.

THERE WAS AN OLD ZEN MASTER in China who would wake up each morning and shout, "Master!" and then answer himself, "Yes, Master?" Then he'd say, "Don't be deceived, Master!" and then reply, "No, Master, I won't!"

That's true understanding of authority.

"PASS ME the ECSTASY, RAINBOW, I'M GOING ō NIRVANA ᴼᴺ STRETCHER!"

Can you hear that, dude? That's my
skull! I'm so wasted!
JEFF SPICOLI (PLAYED BY SEAN PENN)
IN FAST TIMES AT RIDGEMONT HIGH
ENJOYING A HEIGHTENED STATE OF AWARENESS

U NTIL RECENTLY I was naïve enough to believe that the idiotic notion that taking drugs was somehow a legitimate path toward Buddhist enlightenment had gone out of fashion long ago—about the time The Velvet Underground recorded their final album and the last *Star Trek* episode aired with Captain Kirk on the bridge. But when I was in America visiting my parents in July 2002, I was deeply disappointed to find a putrid little book called *Zig Zag Zen* edited by Allan Hunt Badiner taking up a big hunk of shelf space allotted to Buddhism in the local Supermarket 'n' Bookstore.

I picked up that lump of turd and read it. Near as I can come to making any sense out of it, Badiner's argument goes something like this: (A) Buddhism is about enlightenment; (B) enlightenment is some far-out, trippy mystical brain-fuck kind of state; (C) drugs will screw up your brain too; therefore (D) doing drugs will get you enlightened. And besides that, it's much easier to score a hit of acid than it is to sit around staring at walls for years (plus, when you're on acid the blank walls look *so much more far out, man*).

Badiner believes that we *must* address the issue of how Buddhism and drugs are related because lots of Westerners who went on to become Buddhist masters—like me, for example—used drugs in their early years (as did lots of people who went on to become career criminals—but let's leave that aside). According to Badiner, these Buddhist masters' youthful drug abuse is "Western Buddhism's deep, dark secret." Most Buddhist teachers who've used drugs in the past have gone on to say that they are dangerous at worst and a waste of time at best—and in any case certainly unrelated to Buddhism. Yet, Badiner believes, the enlightenment those guys found in Buddhism was the same whacked-out state of mind they got from dope.

In fact, drugs occupy exactly the same place in Western Buddhism as Gautama Buddha's early experiments with severe asceticism. Before he discovered the Middle Way, Gautama tried all kinds of weird-ass stuff to attain enlightenment, including starving himself nearly to death. He saw that although ascetic practices could give him that same tripped-out feeling you can get when doing some really primo shit, none of that got him any closer to understanding the truth or stopping suffering. He gave it up and spent the rest of his career putting those practices down.

A number of *Zig Zag Zen*'s contributors point out that various sects that claim to be Buddhist use techniques such as physical exhaustion, food and sleep deprivation, and various kinds of mental gymnastics to achieve changes in brain chemistry similar to the ones you get from the stuff you can buy from the sleazebags slouching around down by the nine-year-old girls at the playground. True enough. But those practices are not Buddhism, no matter how venerable and traditional the guys hawking them appear to be. It's a sad fact that far too many of those who claim to be Buddha's followers indulge in the sort of practices the Buddha himself clearly and unambiguously condemned.

And then there is the little problem of the fifth precept—the one in which Buddha explicitly told his followers not to do drugs. In *Zig Zag Zen*, Badiner takes great pains to point out the distinction between what he calls "consciousness-restricting drugs" and what he calls "entheogens," drugs he believes give you real spiritual experiences. Perhaps we're to believe that Buddha's prohibition refers only to certain crappy drugs, and that we're free to get toasted on the good stuff. But Buddha used a word that translates as "intoxicants," thus making no such distinction possible. And FYI: the ancient Indians may not have had LSD or "E," but they knew all about naturally occurring psychedelics. This distinction, however, has a significant flaw, and by "significant" I mean "large enough to drive a '72 Buick LeSabre through." Consider this:

> 1. Would you ride in a car whose driver was on the consciousness-expanding "entheogenic" drug LSD?

And here's a bonus question:

> 2. Why does an "expanded consciousness" include the inability to operate a motor vehicle?

One of the few contributors to the book who even acknowledges the fifth precept, Dokusho Vallalba *Sensei*,* thinks doing drugs is fine if the "setting" is correct. But in my experience such a "setting" almost always includes one person who stays straight and looks after the safety of the drug-user. Now, just why is it that people at higher levels of consciousness can't seem to survive without one of us low-level folks there to help them out? Those of you who've ever been that caretaker know just how much fun

---

*SENSEI is a mild Japanese honorific that can refer to anyone from a preschool teacher to a hairdresser.

it can be to try and keep folks in "heightened states of awareness" from doing themselves grievous bodily harm.

The very good reason most Western Buddhist teachers don't talk much about the druggy days of their youth is because there are always guys around who'll latch onto any little scrap to justify their own predilection for getting wasted. *Zig Zag Zen* contributor Rick Fields cites the story—probably apocryphal—of how Nagarjuna, one of Buddhism's most brilliant poet-philosophers, told one of his disciples to accept only whatever food could fit on the end of a pin. The disciple came back with a pancake balanced on a pin. Fields calls this "compelling evidence" that Nagarjuna's real source of inspiration was magic mushrooms—since, y'know, a mushroom sorta looks a little like a pancake balanced on top of a pin if you think about it hard enough (especially if your thinking about it while tripped out on 'shrooms). So while I'm personally reluctant to drag those skeletons out of my own closet, the existence of *Zig Zag Zen* and its dubious claims of being the first work to take a serious look at the matter make me feel it's necessary to address what really shouldn't even be an issue at all.

LIKE SO MANY OTHER pimply-faced young Buddhist wanna-bes in the West, when I was a boneheaded little college dweeb I was dumb enough to fall for the spiel of one of these irresponsible pricks who claimed that psychedelic drugs were one of the "skillful means" spoken of in Buddhist literature for reaching enlightenment.

Now in high school, I was a major fan of John Lennon and knew Lennon had used LSD so I really wanted to try it for myself. Hell, I would've posed naked with Yoko Ono if it'd have made me more like John Lennon.* One morning,

----

*I have realized since then that Yoko was the real genius in their collaborations, and Yoko, if you're reading this, I'd still love to pose naked with you.

probably late in my junior year, a friend and I found a dealer in the school parking lot—which was a veritable drug supermarket at the time—who sold us what he said was acid. We went to my friend's treehouse that night and each swallowed one of the pills we'd bought. We waited and waited, but nothing happened. We'd been scammed. We were more relieved than angry though. Oddly enough, a few days later, when I confronted the guy who'd sold the pills to us, he just laughed and gave the money back. Honor among thieves, I suppose.

Once I joined Zero Defex, I became aware that LSD—*real* LSD, that is—might be available. I knew Jimi Imij, our singer, had used it. He was a great acid-head philosopher, always willing to hold forth with psychedelic cosmic wisdom. I asked him once if it was true you could see God when you took acid. "Yeah," he said, "but you can see the Devil too."

At that time, though, I didn't ask him for any LSD because I was in a heavy anti-drug phase. I'd given up John Lennon (and my hopes for Yoko) and the whole hippy thing and embraced punk. Whatever the hippies were for, punk was against. One of the things that really got me interested in Zero Defex in the first place was their anti-drug stance. They had a song called "The Drug Song" whose chorus went, "Your drugs suck, don't push them on me!" Tommy Strange, our guitarist, used to drink beer though. Our drummer might have joined him sometimes. Jimi Imij didn't use any drugs at the time, as far as I could tell, and neither did I. We were aghast when the Meat Puppets came through town with bags full of pot. *Hippies! Sell-outs!**

A lot of people in our scene were into Straight Edge, a movement spearheaded by the Washington, D.C., band, Minor Threat, and their singer Ian MacKaye. Straight Edgers didn't drink, didn't smoke, didn't do drugs, and

---

*Great band, though. They blew us off stage that night.

claimed to renounce meaningless sex as well. They liked
to draw big **X**'s on their hands with Magic Marker, an imitation of the mark minors got at "all-ages" shows held at
bars. I admired the Straight Edgers and although I also did-
n't do the things they didn't do, I wasn't into joining move-
ments and never called myself Straight Edge (plus, when I
refrained from meaningless sex in those days, it was
because I didn't have any other choice).

In spite of my anti-drug stance, though, my interest in
trying out the psychedelic experience remained. When
Zero Defex broke up and I got into the burgeoning garage/
psychedelic revival scene, I virtually lost myself in the
new '60s. The music, clothes, and trends of the '80s were
repulsive, and everything from the '60s seemed so much
cooler.

Ram Dass's book *Be Here Now* became my bible. I used
to carry that thing with me wherever I went. But in spite of
the book's wonderfully profound title, *Be Here Now* is also
a huge, flashing neon advertisement for drugs. Just like *Zig
Zag Zen* will no doubt be for kids today, *Be Here Now* was,
for me, just what I needed to legitimize my desire to get
zonked out of my skull and pretend it was a religious experience. Now all I had to do was get my hands on the goods.

In the spring of 1984, Bill, the rhythm guitar player with
The F-Models and one of the guys with whom I was sharing a horrible old house near the Kent State campus, got
hold of some acid blotter and shared it with me. It was
pretty much your standard acid trip. The rug moved. Time
became distorted. When I waved my hand in front of my
face I saw a whole trail of hands waving there just like
those pictures of Hindu gods.

I did have one insight on drugs—though it made no difference whatsoever in anything about my life or anyone
else's. I was alone in what had once been the house's living
room, but which now just had a rotten old couch and a

black-and-white TV set no one ever watched. As I sat there
the thought suddenly occurred to me, "This is it." This,
what I was living through right then and there—not the
drug-induced state, mind you, but my plain old existence as
a twenty-year-old white male human being on planet Earth
was all there was for me. I was shocked and frightened by
the prospect and did everything I could to put it out of my
mind as quickly as possible. I turned on the TV and tuned
it to a nonbroadcasting channel to watch the static, an
activity I'd heard was supposed to be pretty groovy when
you're on acid. And it was groovy, man. I saw all kinds of
things happening in that static.

I took two more trips that summer and they were neither very good nor very bad, but they never delivered anything close to the beatific vision Ram Dass had promised.
The next one, though, was a nightmare of epic proportions.

This guy Donnel, an Irish grad student who also lived at
the house with Bill and me, had procured some acid from a
somewhat shady source (as if there is any other kind...but
this source was particularly iffy). The blotter was purple
and Donnel had been warned that it was very strong. I figured I could handle it. What I didn't know was that Donnel
chased his hit with a full quart of whiskey and then, decid-
ing one extra-strong hit of dodgy purple blotter might not
be enough for the night, had swallowed another one as well.

This stuff was definitely strong and very speedy. We were
all wired to the gills as well as stoned. I was actually hallu-
cinating—the first time that had happened. Whenever I
closed my eyes the patterns on my eyelids formed into
bizarre shapes. I couldn't shut out my vision. I started to get
tense. I kept telling myself that the drug would wear off in
a few hours. But, as hard as I tried I could not get any sense
of what "a few hours" meant. How the hell long was a few
hours? What was an hour? How could it have "length"? I
understood that the position of the hands of my watch

meant that it was one A.M. What "one A.M." meant, however, I had no clue. The word *hour* might as well have been an unknown word in a foreign language. I turned it over and over in my mind. But as hard as I tried I couldn't make anything out of it at all. I had completely forgotten the concept of time. This was terror piled upon terror. I knew I'd be well in a few hours *but what for the love of God was an hour?*

I went to the toilet, afraid to be alone, and took a shaky piss. I went to wash my hands and, looking up at the cracked mirror, discovered that looking into mirrors was not such a good idea. My face was changing, melting into a bizarre array of ever evolving shapes, most of them weird and ugly.

After considerable effort I managed to stop panicking. I went into the kitchen to chill out. Just then Donnel showed up again. He'd disappeared a few hours before (or a few minutes, I wouldn't have known the difference), apparently to chug down more whiskey. When he arrived in the kitchen, I was wadding up pieces of tinfoil and tossing them into the garbage can. It was distracting me from the sudden flashes of naked horror that kept threatening to tear my brain apart. Donnel decided he wanted to play too. But instead of wadding up a ball of tinfoil, he wrenched the door off the oven and tossed it across the room, shouting, "Why don't we just throw it all away!"

After I came down I vowed never to touch LSD again.

DRUGS ARE EXTREMELY DESTRUCTIVE to your physical body, and they can leave emotional psychic wounds that can form permanent scars. They do not aid you in usefully discovering the truth in the least. I'm amazed I even survived my experimentation with that poison. My advice to you: Don't bother.

The only lasting value in the acid experience for me was the clear understanding that acid wasn't going to live up to the promises of guys like Ram Dass and Allan Hunt Badiner. It also left me wondering how those guys could be so stupid as not to notice that for themselves. If that's beatific vision and ultimate truth, they can keep it.

Any kind of traumatic experience—a car accident, a high fever, the death of a loved one—can dramatically rip a person out of their normal consciousness. But psychedelic drugs mangle your brain and body and when you start off with the idea that some mangled, abnormal state of mind is the "optimal state of consciousness," as *Zig Zag Zen* postulates in its first chapter, the boneheaded notion that getting bombed out of your gourd is the way to find reality is a pretty easy conclusion to jump to. But if there is one thing I want to make clear, it's that Buddhism has nothing to do with "transcendent states" or "higher levels of consciousness" or "optimal levels of being." (I remain unconvinced, by the way, that a state of mind where you can no longer even roll your own doobies, let alone do anything the least bit useful for anyone else, is somehow "optimal.")

Buddhism isn't about anything so diminutive as any of your mental states at all. It's much deeper than that.

There is no optimal state of consciousness. Optimal is just an idea, another manifestation of the Great Somewhere Else. Consciousness is just an idea.

The notion that you can take a drug to get enlightened is as sensible as thinking you can take off the weight gained from twenty years of shoveling nothing but Oreos®, Pringles®, and Big Macs® down your gullet by swallowing a few miracle diet pills. It's big money for big business, but if you're eating three meals a day at Mickey D's you're gonna be taking up two seats on a 747 regardless of how many pills you pop.

Incredibly, the belief that a lifetime—hundreds of thousands lifetimes, since our consciousness includes the acquired cultural and social knowledge of our entire species' history—of bad thinking habits can be altered in a single evening high on LSD continues to be talked about seriously by people who really ought to know better. In *Zig Zag Zen*, Terence McKenna even comes out with the comically ridiculous question, "How can you be a serious Buddhist if you're not doing psychedelics?" This kind of thing is a lot like eloquent discourse on tantric sex from guys who really only want to get their rocks off more often and better.

If you want to get fried off your ass, at least have the decency to admit it. Don't try to convince us you're on some kind of grand spiritual quest.

Drugs won't show you the truth.

Drugs will only show you what it's like to be on drugs.

ONCE TIM TOLD ME the story of how one of his teacher Kobun Chino's students slipped him some acid. Kobun was a very trusting guy. When he was handed an acid-soaked sugar cube and told, "Here, eat this. It'll make you feel good," Kobun swallowed it without a second thought. His comments afterward about the LSD experience? "It was stupid," he said. Spoken like a true Zen master.

The very idea of higher states of consciousness is absurd. Comparing one state of consciousness to another and saying one is "higher" and the other is "mundane" is like eating a banana and complaining it's not a very good apple. The state of consciousness you have right now is 100 percent purely what it is. It is neither higher nor lower, better or worse, more or less significant, than the state of consciousness once achieved by some spaced-out swami who came back down and then wrote a book about his memories of it.

Are the visions you can experience on LSD "real" religious visions? Sure they are. And as such they are worse than useless. Religious visions and acid experiences are both fantasies, delusions, projections of your own hidden desires. They have nothing whatsoever to do with the truth, nothing to do with reality. You learn even less about the true nature of reality from such fantasies than from watching a few hours of cartoons on Saturday morning.

Chasing after fantasies is always a bad idea. Stick with reality. Reality's all you've got.

But here's the real secret, the real miracle: It's enough.

EATING A TANGERINE ⇄ REAL ENLIGHTENMENT

Hmm... eternal happiness for a dollar?
I'd rather keep the dollar.
MONTGOMERY BURNS ON THE SIMPSONS

DRUGS AREN'T THE ONLY WAY to alter your consciousness and send you out chasing fantasies. Sometimes meditation does the trick just as well.

Once this guy who objected strongly to my oddball ways of presenting Buddhism sent me a piece by Ken Wilber, an enormously popular writer of Buddhist-style books (apparently)—though I'd never heard of him. Wilber, in this guy's opinion, represented Real Truth as opposed to the drivel I put out. He wanted me to see the light.

In the piece my friend sent me, we learn that Wilber had read a phrase by Ramana Maharshi, an Indian teacher whose philosophy sometimes resembles Zen although he never studied Zen. The phrase was this: "That which is not present in deep, dreamless sleep is not real." This phrase, Wilber says, deeply affected him and made him *truly serious* about meditation.

Wilber then tells of how he trained himself to be conscious even during deep sleep. He brags that he spent some *eleven days straight* in this condition during a retreat at a monastery.

If you do zazen long enough, this kind of stuff can happen. It's a kind of sickness. And one of the good effects of getting sick is that when you recover you see just how nice your regular condition is. Good teachers can help you get over this illness; bad teachers will just let you get sicker and sicker. Some of the most dangerous ones even encourage it, writing books with their handsome mug on the cover filled with twisted explanations that being sick is really the only true way to be healthy.

Being conscious during sleep states isn't anything to get too excited about. Delusions that exist during the day don't disappear when you shut your eyes. In fact, they often get far worse.

The problem with Wilber was that the poor guy mistook this special condition, this sickness, for enlightenment. Any kind of enlightenment that requires some mystical state is worse than useless. It just reinforces the belief that your "self" has some kind of objective reality. Who's going to have this exalted state of "heightened consciousness"? Who's going to float in the formless state of "no up, no down, no over and no there" Wilber claims to have discovered? Who's going to become enlightened? Why it's "you" of course!—your self-important self-existent selfish self!

I'LL TELL YOU, THOUGH, when I read this piece I was initially suckered by it. Wilber is a very persuasive writer—hypnotic and positively seductive. When you find yourself getting sucked in by something like that, you've got to take a step back, breathe a little, and see what your intuitions tell you. Does reading these things make you notice your own real life here and now? Or does it reinforce a fantasy about going off to exotic places to experience mysterious and wonderful altered states of consciousness—so very much higher than the mundane consciousness you've actually got? Does that kind of writing clarify your own inherent perfection or just draw attention the specialness of the author's insights and experiences?

You've been deceiving yourself for millions of years; it's what your brain evolved to do. But once you catch sight of balance and learn where the center is, you can use your brain differently and always find that center, that balance, and that true reality again in any moment.

Those eleven days of whacked-out *über*-consciousness must have been quite an adventure for Wilber. And adventures are fun. But after any adventure you've always got to come back home, back to the drab, dull, ordinary work-a-day world.

Why is that? This is a very important question: *Why is your lame-ass, ordinary work-a-day life the one you keep coming back to?* Why is it you always, always, always end up right back here no matter how far out or how high up you get?

The fact is, the universe has chosen you as the vehicle through which to experience the uncanny thrill of cutting up cabbage for dinner, the wonder that is inhaling oxygen and exhaling carbon dioxide, the fabulous spectacle of watching your clothes dry at a coin-op Laundromat™ where the radio is stuck on an EZ-listening station and an old lady keeps staring at you for no discernible reason. The universe has demanded that you be you. Ain't no avoidin' it.

What is true during dreamless sleep is true no matter whether you can recall the experience and write about it or not. What is true in a whorehouse in Bangkok is true whether you visit it and take Polaroids or not. What is true for six-legged aliens on the fifth planet circling Epsilon Centauri is true whether you go there and talk to them or not. You may never know the life your toothbrush leads when you're not around but it's certainly real.

There's a personal reason this particular piece of Wilber's writing had such an effect on me and why I'm spending all this ink writing about it now: It mirrors an experience of my own that was very important in clarifying for me one of the most vital points of Buddhist teaching.

ABOUT A YEAR AFTER my experience by the Sengawa River, I started to have some weird experiences in my sleep, a lot like Wilber's (though this was years before I read his piece). I wrote down the first one of mine a few hours after it happened:

> I woke up this morning around 3 or 4. It was raining hard and the sound must have woken me. There was this strange feeling then, like a gigantic open space. I had the feeling that there was no one at all in the room, just the sound of the rain and some kind of movement. No personality at all. I couldn't understand the feeling, so I sat up to be sure I was really awake. After a while I went back to sleep. When I woke up again with the 6:30 alarm, the feeling had ended.

Very cool, huh? Very mystical and far out. But it didn't stop there…

I'm not sure how many nights later The Big One hit. Maybe a couple weeks. Maybe a month. It started off with coming to full awareness while deeply asleep. It wasn't a lucid dream. I've had so many of those I'm used to them by now. This was something entirely different. I was actually aware of that open formless state of deep dreamless sleep.

Real trippy, doncha think? And it gets even better. Soon I found myself surveying the entire universe much as God himself might do. I could perceive the whole of all creation all at once. I don't say I "saw" it because I didn't seem to have any eyes or any body. Or rather, the universe *itself* was my body and mind. I perceived galactic clusters and massive star formations the way I normally perceive my own arms and legs. Or something. It's impossible to describe.

The universe was evolving before me. I was aware that millions of years were passing, yet I was experiencing them as mere moments. Again, description is impossible. Whatever. I saw the universe coming together. First one planet became unified into a single being. Not just the intelligent species but all life-forms on the planet and ultimately the planet itself. This spread through the planet's solar system and then on to other solar systems nearby. Meanwhile the same thing was happening in other parts of the universe millions of lightyears away. The unified sections gradually met each other and became bigger and bigger. Finally the entire universe consisted of just two "beings" composed of the combined matter and space of a billion, trillion, Godzillian galaxies.

The two beings faced each other, and I, now one of those beings, felt exactly as I do when I face my wife. And we melted into each other. The whole universe, stretching on into infinite time and infinite space, was now one single unified being. No tension. No fear. No competition.

But the universe was lonely. There was no one to talk to. No one to share its experience with. No *other*. And with no other to contrast to, no self. To cure its loneliness it split into two again, then four, six, eight, and on and on until, over a period of billions upon billions of millennia it was back to being countless individual beings. At that point I felt myself swept back into my own body once more. I opened my eyes and I was in my bed.

IT'S DIFFICULT TO CONVEY the sheer power of this vision. Reading it back now, it just sounds like a really weird dream or a fair-to-middling science fiction story. But it was utterly real to me. As real as any experience I've ever had in my life. Realer.

Unlike what happened after my Sengawa River experience, I was in a daze following this one. It was difficult to
concentrate on such trivia as work when I'd seen the whole
history of the universe from the point of view of God.

I wasn't sure what to make of what had happened. In all
the time I'd spent listening to lectures by Nishijima and
Tim they'd never described anything like merging with the
mind of God and watching the beginning and end of the
universe unfold. Dogen never wrote about anything like
that in the *Shobogenzo*. Buddha himself never spoke of
such things. Yet I was certain the experience had been real.

Finally I screwed up my nerve and decided to tell Nishijima about it. There were some things going on that prevented me from seeing him face-to-face just then, so I wrote
him a long e-mail describing everything in minute detail. I
don't know what I expected to hear back from him. Perhaps
a fatherly, "Yes, my son, you have glimpsed the secret
truth. But you must never speak of it to others, for only
when they are ready shall they learn of such things."

But that wasn't what he said.

He sent me back an e-mail the next day saying that what
I experienced was just a fantasy. It would "never come true
even in the future." Furthermore, he said that someone like
me who worked "in the animation business"* needs to be
more realistic.

I was devastated.

Why couldn't he understand? This wasn't a fantasy! This
was true! It had nothing to do with my working in "the animation business." This was serious and deeply profound.
Come on! *Merging With The Mind Of God!* How can you
get any deeper and more profound?

I nearly cried as I read his e-mail to me. I'm sure I would
have broken down if he'd said that to me in person. I spent

*Which I don't—but that's beside the point.

the whole morning just feeling sorry and confused. It was a huge come-down. There could be none more huge.

BUT AS THE DAY WORE ON, I began to notice a few things that I'd been too stupid to suss out for the past few weeks. For one thing, if your experience of enlightenment is real, no one can ever take it from you or deny it. Enlightenment means manifesting truly what you really are at every moment. No amount of criticism from anyone can ever take that away any more than someone's critical words could somehow magically make your nose disappear.* No one can take you away from you.

But my big experience of merging with God, however profound and moving it was at the time, was in the past. It wasn't here and it wasn't now. In fact, the memory was so powerful it was standing in the way of my real experience of here and now. I was sacrificing my real, everyday existence for a dream. Whether I really experienced the beginning and end of the universe or not was entirely beside the point. It didn't matter right now because right now that was not what I was experiencing. I was experiencing being a formerly elated guy sitting at his desk in an office in Tokyo feeling sorry for himself. What happened that night was gone. Gone like the day I received the Buddhist precepts, gone like the day I first heard the Heart Sutra, gone like every gig Zero Defex ever played, gone like my first kiss was gone, gone like my childhood in Nairobi was gone. Gone, gone, gone, never to return no matter how much I wished, grieved, or fantasized.

This kind of thing is a common problem among zazen practitioners. They have these really cool experiences, or really cutting insights, and then they latch onto them forever, like a pitbull onto a postman's ass—effectively missing

---

*"Got yer enlightenment!"

out on the rest of their lives. It's a game the ego plays: if it can't keep you believing in it through all the usual methods, it tosses something that feels just like what you always imagined enlightenment ought to feel like. Once you start believing in that stuff your ego's got you right where it wants you. You'll never be able to look at your day-to-day life honestly again.

But you've got to forget all of that stuff and get back to where you are.

BY LUNCHTIME I'd been mulling over Nishijima's e-mail for a couple hours and I just felt kind of doomed to trudge through the rest of my dumb, sad, sorry little life.

But there was something else twinkling at the edge of my mind. I knew my life wasn't really bad at all. It was a lovely thing. It was a precious, fragile, and very valuable thing. There are many diamonds in the world and if you lose your favorite, you can work hard, earn a lot of money and get another one to replace it. But the moments of your life aren't like that. Once they're gone, they'll never return. Each and every one is the most precious thing in existence. You can never meaningfully compare one moment with any other. You can never meaningfully compare your life with anyone else's. No matter how rich someone else may be, no matter how happy they look, no matter how enlightened they seem, they can never be you. Never, ever, ever.

Only you can live your life.

My wife had given me a *mikan*, a kind of Japanese tangerine, for lunch that day—and I sat at my desk and started to peel it. As I watched the peel come free from the fruit, I was struck by how beautiful it was. It was one tangerine, perfect in its own way. The orange color leapt out at me, as if it was glowing from the inside, brighter than a neon light. The intensity of its beauty was almost painful to me. I've seen some beautiful sights in my life: sunset over the Pacific from the western shore of Maui, Mount Kilimanjaro rising above the plain as elephants and giraffes saunter by in the foreground, the tranquil dignity of ancient Buddhist temples. But at that moment nothing could compare to that little tangerine in my hands. I felt so grateful just to be me, just to be sitting at my desk, just to be able to peel and taste and eat that tangerine. No one else would ever taste that tangerine.

When I got back home I sent Nishijima another e-mail telling him about the tangerine and thanking him for setting me straight. The next day I got his reply: "Eating a tangerine is real enlightenment." It was something he really didn't need to say. Still, I was glad he did.

I FEEL SORRY FOR KEN WILBER and other folk like him. I really do. Maybe I shouldn't—since Ken's far richer and way more famous than I'll ever be. But either he never had a teacher who told him the truth, or if he did he missed it and chose to dwell in his own fantasies instead. At the same time, I understand his situation. I could easily have gone down that same road: Had Nishijima confirmed my experience of Oneness With God as "real enlightenment," I would've been sucked right in. I could've stayed that way for years, I'm sure, possibly forever. Or I could have followed my initial feeling upon reading Nishijima's e-mail and rejected what he said. I could have decided Nishijima was obviously less enlightened than I believed him to be, and less enlightened than I clearly now was. It would've been no trouble at all to find another teacher who'd have confirmed my experience. Or I could've dispensed with teachers altogether and just decided to start building up my own cult of personal hero-worshipers, all striving to have the same supercool experience I had had.

But I couldn't really do any of those things because I knew better and I had to be honest with myself about it.

It's a frightening thing to be truly honest with yourself. It means you have no one left to turn to anymore, no one to blame, and to one to look to for salvation. You have to give up any possibility that there will ever be any refuge for you. You have to accept the reality that you are truly and finally on your own. The best thing you can hope for in life is to meet a teacher who will smash all of your dreams, dash all of your hopes, tear your teddy-bear beliefs out of your arms and fling them over a cliff.

WHY IS IT that we prefer fantasies to what our life really is? If some great "enlightened being" tells us what his life is like, why shouldn't we aspire to that instead? What's the difference between Wilber telling us that he floats forever free in the sea of "no up and no down," and me telling you about my experience by Sengawa River or my assertion that there really is no "self"?

If you really want to know the answers to these questions, you have to examine your own life very closely and with complete honesty. And you have to find out for yourself.

People are very much alike. Our brains are all similar in a very deep way. What appeals to one person will pretty much appeal at some level to just about anyone else. Certain fantasies are universal and very compelling—like the Coca-Cola® of our minds, flavors that tap something so basic it's hard to find anyone who doesn't like them at least a little.

These basic human fantasies have been with us since our species first arose. Stories that tap into these fantasies have tremendous power to appeal to huge numbers of people. But the truth is more powerful. Always.

So the question becomes this: How do we know what is true and what is fantasy?

And the answer: Take a look at where you are, at who you are, right here and right now. That's it. That's the truth.

HARDCORE ZEN

You ain't no punk, you punk.
You wanna talk about the real junk?
"GARBAGEMAN" BY THE CRAMPS
FROM THE ALBUM BAD MUSIC FOR BAD PEOPLE

ZEN IS A PHILOSOPHY OF ACTION. That means it isn't just a philosophy you read about and think about. It's a philosophy you *do*. You can't possibly truly understand Zen Buddhism without practicing zazen.

It's not enough to read about it. It's not even enough to understand it. You have to live it.

So why don't more people do it? The scholars, the armchair masters, the people who love the *idea* of meditation, but who just can't commit to actually doing it—why don't they sit zazen? In *Zig Zag Zen*, psychologist Charles Tart says, "It's clear that many of us Westerners have such hyperactive minds and complex psychological dynamics that it is very difficult to quiet and discipline our minds enough to make any real progress along the meditative path."

"Westerners can't meditate" is a favorite excuse for not doing zazen—but man, I hate racism especially when it pretends to be rational and philosophical. In Japan, where they obviously can't use this excuse, folks like to believe that only priests can do zazen, that other folks are somehow unqualified.

Another excuse I hear is that modern people just "don't have the time" for it. Why would you want to waste time sitting on a cushion staring at a wall when there are so many "important" things you could be doing, like watching a rerun of *The Simpsons*, logging on to the internet to see if anything crucial has been added since this morning, or hanging out getting into a condition you'll regret the next day?

You may be busy with work and family and responsibilities and all that, I sure am, but I'll bet you also waste a hell of a lot of time every day. You devote hours and hours each week to "relaxing" in ways that aren't relaxing in the least. You kill time. You steal a nap. You screw off.

If you were bound and gagged inside a wooden barrel just about to head over Niagara Falls, you'd pray for just one minute more to live. And yet, while you're alive, what do you do? You get bored. You wish to be elsewhere. You wish to get whatever you're doing now over with. You want to speed by those boring minutes like your life is a video where you can fast-forward through the commercials. When the end comes you'll be wishing you could have back all those boring moments you zipped through. But you killed them. Dead and gone. Try putting some of that time to good use and see what happens.

The fact is, the great Eastern masters of times gone-by are no different from you. Their minds were just as hyperactive as yours and their psychological dynamics every bit as complex. The heights of enlightenment they reached are absolutely accessible to you. This stuff is tough work for anybody, regardless of where they were born or when. Cut out just a bit of those empty distractions and see how much time you create.

TIM ONCE TOLD ME A STORY about Kobun Chino leading a zazen practice. Kobun showed up late and everyone else in the room was already doing zazen. Kobun came in, sat down, looked around at everyone diligently practicing, chuckled and said, "What a stupid thing to do." Then he rang the bell signaling the start of the zazen period.

No doubt about it, though, zazen is a stupid thing to do.

Zazen is also boring. You couldn't possibly find a duller practice.

And you don't have to do it at all, but if you decide you want to try it, here's how.

It couldn't be simpler, actually. Go to a quiet place. It doesn't need to be completely silent, but quieter is often better, at least in the beginning. A fairly bright room is good, because it tends to prevent dozing off. Find yourself a cushion to sit on. Take one off your couch or use your bed pillow. Rolled up blankets do nicely, too. Fold or fluff or do whatever you need to make your cushion a few inches high, just enough to lift your butt off the ground and tilt your pelvis downward a little. Sit on it facing a blank undecorated wall. Cross your legs in front of you. If you know how to do the full-lotus or half-lotus positions, and you really feel like it, you can twist your legs up like that.

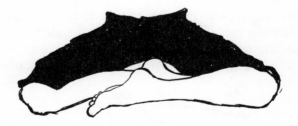

Modified Cross-Legged Position

If you can manage the full-lotus, this is the most "stable" position. If these positions don't feel comfortable, don't do them. Just sit in a modified version of what we used to call Indian-style with your legs loosely crossed and your ankles flat on the floor. The most important thing is to make your spine straight. It should feel as if your vertebrae are balanced on top of each other. Find a position where you are using as little energy as possible to maintain

The Complete Posture

your erect spine. You want to balance all your meat and bones on top of your pelvis. Now tilt your head down slightly, tucking your chin in a bit.

The traditional hand-position is what's called the *universal mudra*.

The Universal Mudra

You put your hands together facing palms-up at about belly-button level, then make a little circle with your thumbs together on top. The advantage of the full- or half-lotus posture here is that you can use your feet like a little table to rest your hands on when doing the mudra. Rest your wrists on the tops of your thighs.

Now sit there and breathe normally, not real deep, not real shallow. Not fast, not slow. Just let it go on, in and out. Don't make any effort to stop your thoughts. But if you find yourself drifting off into some reverie, straighten your spine. In all my years of sitting, I've never found myself drifting off without my spine going correspondingly slack or out of alignment. When your posture is right, thoughts slow by themselves. Or they don't. And if they don't, don't worry too much. Just keep on sitting.

You may find that your legs fall asleep. No big deal. If that happens you can do one of two things: not worry about it and just take your time standing up after zazen, so you don't fall over, or you can shift your legs a little. Personally, I shift my legs and get back to zazen. Just be careful you don't spend your entire time shifting around.

If you've absolutely gotta scratch, scratch. If you've absolutely gotta fix your legs cuz you're just in excruciating pain or something, fix your legs. Whatever stuff like that needs doing, do it with as little fuss as possible and return to the position. But also experiment with not worrying about all that so much. Do this for as long as you can stand it, but no more than forty-five minutes at a stretch. And consistency on a day-to-day basis is far more important than duration at any one time.

Morning is the best time for zazen but evenings are also good. Twenty minutes in the morning and twenty before bed is good for starters. I try to put in an hour a day, but I'm a gung-ho kinda guy.

This style of zazen is traditionally called *shikantaza*, or "just sitting." This is the real deal, sisters and brothers. This is hardcore Zen. There are other forms of meditation where you're given objects to concentrate on, mantras to recite, special ways of breathing and so on. There are practices that grade certain levels of concentration, leading students from the lowest levels up to the most exalted. There are temples where they come around and whack you with a stick if they think you're not sitting right. Hardcore Zen isn't like that. Everything non-essential has been stripped away. That other stuff is like swimming with Water-Wings® or riding a bike with training wheels. You won't really learn to balance on your bike until you take the training wheels off, and you'll never learn how to keep yourself afloat if you don't you ditch the Water-Wings®. When you're ready for the real thing, you've gotta lose the props. No two ways about it.

The practice of zazen has to be approached with care. Remember those demons I told you about? You've got 'em too. And if you're not careful they can do real damage. If things start getting a little too heavy, back off for a while. Stop doing zazen if it really starts to bug you. Or seek out a good teacher or even a therapist if that's your thing.

Probably, though, zazen will just be boring.

But as simple as zazen is, it's best to have a teacher. Your teacher is a friend who can help you deal with the things that come up during the practice. Good ones aren't that hard to find. The best Zen teachers don't go making fools of themselves by writing books, like me. They're mostly quiet, unassuming folks with little groups. Don't worry whether the teacher you find is going to be the Best In The World or not. Go and see what he or she is all about. If it's not right, you'll work that out soon enough.

Sit zazen.

And rest assured, by sitting staring at blank walls you can transform everything. *Everything.* This is not a metaphor. This is not exaggeration. This is the simple fact of the matter.

ZEN REPLACES ALL OBJECTS OF BELIEF with one single thing: reality itself. We believe only in this universe. We don't believe in the afterlife. We don't believe in the sovereignty of nations. We don't believe in money or power or fame. We don't believe in our idols. We don't believe in our positions or our possessions. We don't believe we can be insulted, or that our honor or the honor of our family, our nation or our faith can be offended. We don't believe in Buddha.

We just believe in reality. Just this.

Zen doesn't ask you to believe in anything you cannot confirm for yourself. It does not ask you to memorize any sacred words. It doesn't require you to worship any particular thing or revere any particular person. It doesn't offer any rules to obey. It doesn't give you any hierarchy of learned men whose profound teachings you must follow to the letter. It doesn't ask you to conform to any code of dress. It doesn't ask you to allow anyone else to choose what is right for you and what is wrong.

Zen is the complete absence of belief. Zen is the complete lack of authority. Zen tears away every false refuge in which you might hide from the truth and forces you to sit naked before what is real. That's real refuge.

Reality will announce itself to you in utterly unmistakable ways once you learn to listen. Learning to listen to reality, though, ain't so easy. You're so used to shouting reality down, drowning it out completely with your own opinions and views, that you might not even be able to recognize reality's voice anymore. It's a funny thing, though, because reality is the single most glaringly obvious thing there is. As the woman said in those old Palmolive® commercials, "You're soaking in it!" Yet we've forgotten how to recognize it.

All your life you learned to deal with reality by excluding certain things, dividing things up into categories, differentiating between this and that. But reality includes all those things we call "wrong," all those things we call "evil," all those things we hate because we know in our hearts they are bad things. We can only know what's "bad" when we discover it within ourselves and label it as such. But what happens is that we establish psychological blinders that prevent us from even seeing that what we consider bad is part of our own psychological makeup. To face reality as it is means we must face even the bad things about ourselves, the things we desperately want to believe are not there because we so desperately want to cling to the idea that we are "good."

And knowing what's really within us, we must still practice being good. Practicing Buddhism means being aware of what's here and now. And that ain't easy.

The word *Buddhism* means a lot of things to a lot of people—stuff like the *Tibetan Book of the Dead*, those Vietnamese guys who burned themselves on the street in the '60s, and the Aum Shinri Kyo cult who gassed the Tokyo subways. For Japanese people, Buddhism means funerals and temples and the popular TV image of monks standing naked under waterfalls in the middle of the winter.*

Hollywood has turned Buddhism into a lightweight religion full of smiling old bald men spewing meaningless words in voices resonating with authority. Bookstore shelves groan under the weight of trash like *Zig Zag Zen* and a dozen vapid, syrupy tomes with the word *Zen* in the title and some serene image on the cover.

Then there are pop culture's approved list of pseudo-Buddhist masters, people like Ken Wilber, for whom the

---

*I'm not sure who those monks are, though they seem to get a lot of airtime—but that ain't Buddhism.

goal of Buddhism is some imaginary "formless state," or others for whom the "goal" of Buddhism is some fantasy called *satori*. Or Allan Hunt Badiner and the rest of the crew in *Zig Zag Zen*, for whom the goal of Buddhism seems to be to get a really good buzz on.

I once saw a "Buddhist master" who told his students, "I can bring you to full awakening in three years!" And apparently this "full awakening" included sessions in isolation tanks, sky-diving lessons, and vacations in exotic Asian locales—with the students paying for all of the teacher's hotels, food, and travel expenses. Don't ask me how this works, I couldn't follow it either. But that's not Buddhism. It's not even close.

The kinds of fantasies people like this promote are damaging in the extreme. Fantasies of melting into the void, of seeing incredible visions, of achieving peak experiences and making them last forever should be avoided at all costs.

Believe only in the universe as it is right now. See the world and yourself for what they are. Don't be deceived by your imagination no matter how beautiful it is.

Dogen relates a neat story about this in the *Shobogenzo:* A monk's walking around outside and he stubs his toe something fierce. Hopping around in utter agony he thinks, "I've read that pain is void, so what the hell is this?" And all at once he gets it. When his teacher asks him to explain, he says, "I cannot be deceived by others."

We all *want* to be deceived by others. We want to pretend we believe in idiotic philosophies we find comforting. But in the end, no matter how much we try, we can't possibly be deceived. Reality is always there. You can pretend the sky is green with orange polka-dots, but when you open your eyes and look up, it never is.

Zazen will put you directly in touch with the source of yourself. It will bring you into direct contact with something that has never departed from you, something that could never leave you. You can never escape yourself. The truth is always there. Try to look away from it and wherever you turn your head it's right in front of you. Reality is the one and only constant thing in this universe. It's always right there. Just as it is.

EPILOGUE

Cloquet hated reality but realized
it was still the only place to
get a good steak.
WOODY ALLEN

THE WORLD IS CHANGING. Things are getting better. I know that's hard for lots of people to believe, what with terrorism and war and the price of Doc Martens.®

It was hard for me to really see, too. For most of my life I've been the darkest, bleakest most misanthropic pessimist anyone could want to meet (or to avoid, for that matter). I was utterly convinced the world was on the fast track to hell. When I first encountered Nishijima's grinning, sunny optimism I wanted to smack it right off his face.

But here's the thing: You can convince yourself that your pessimistic outlook is "correct" or "realistic" or "justified"—and any newspaper will give you plenty of evidence. You can wallow darkly in your certainty that anyone who sees things in a positive light is an unrealistic empty-headed ninny.

Spend your time doing that and you'll be miserable, which you believe is your right, a personal choice that affects no one but yourself. But it's not. It's an inexcusable way to live because when you live that way you won't do anything about any of what's wrong in the world because, of course, if you succeeded that would prove you were wrong that nothing could be done.

Does letting go of your committed pessimism mean you ignore what's wrong in the world? No. Far from it. Seeing what's wrong and pointing it out is a big part of how you make things better. It is vitally important that you do this.* With weapons of mass destruction within reach of nearly anyone who wants them, you have a duty to make certain that no one in this world ever has any reason to want to use such a thing. This is very much your own personal responsibility. To shirk it isn't just wrong, it's dangerous.

If the world is to change in any important way, that change will come from individual human beings who have the courage to discover who they truly are. And in making this discovery, they will find out what humanity truly is, what the universe truly is. Only people who understand their own nature thoroughly will be able to bring about the changes that must occur if humanity is to survive.

You can transform your life, and it is imperative that you do it. Because only you can do it. No guru can make your life right. No Zen master can show you the way. Only you have the power to make this place you're living in right now a realm so beautiful even God himself couldn't dream of anything better. And doing this will transform the universe.

It is up to you.

It's not just your right; it's your duty.

Only you can find the path and only you can walk it.

To do this, you need to establish balance within yourself. You need a practice that will enable you to see yourself for what you truly are. Zazen is one way you can do that. And zazen can help you establish balance and keep it.

People long for big thrills, peak experiences, deep insights. Some people take up zazen practice expecting that enlightenment will be the ultimate peak experience, the

----

*And I do mean YOU.

peak experience to beat all peak experiences. But real enlightenment is the most ordinary of the ordinary.

And our ordinary, boring, pointless lives are incredibly, amazingly, astoundingly, relentlessly, mercilessly joyful.

You don't need to do a damned thing to experience such joy either. You don't need to snort an ounce of coke, get a turkey-baster full of hot grease shoved up your ass, blow up the Washington Monument, win the Indy 500, or walk on the moon. You don't need to go hang-gliding over the Himalayas, or kayaking down the Amazon. You don't need to screw that oh-so-willing babe with the dark hair and the pouty lips or the smokin' seventeen-year-old on your brother's baseball team, and you don't need to party all night with the beautiful people. You don't need to do any of that stuff to know what it means to be alive.

You're alive when you're sitting in your bedroom cleaning wax out of your ears. You're alive when you're looking at your turds floating in the toilet and noticing bits of last night's dinner in there. You're alive when you're at the supermarket wondering whether to go for the Hostess® Ho-Hos™ or the Little Debbies®. You're alive right now. Just be what you are, where you are. That's the most magical thing there is. The life you're living right now has joys even God could never know.

No one else has ever lived this moment and no one else will ever live it. No one in the whole universe. Oh, there may have been people who stood on subway platforms looking at a book before. But they weren't you. It wasn't this book. They weren't as hungry for a nice slice of pizza as you are right now. They hadn't *schtupped* the people you have. They hadn't made the same stupid mistakes with their lives as you have. Nor have they felt the same joys. They haven't made happy the people you've made happy. The snot in their noses hasn't hardened into the same shapes that the snot in your nose has.

Your life is yours alone, and to miss your life is the most tragic thing that could happen.

So sit down, shut up, and take a look at it.

ACKNOWLEDGMENTS

FIRST AND FOREMOST, I gotta thank the two people who kept telling me I should write a book about Buddhism in spite of my protests that I was supremely unqualified to do any such thing: my current Buddhist teacher, Gudo Wafu Nishijima, and my first teacher, Tim McCarthy. Don't blame me, folks—they made me do it.

Next up, thanks to my editor (I have an editor—cool, huh?) Josh Bartok of Wisdom Publications for making my manuscript into something people might actually want to read. And to Rod Meade Sperry, the guy in charge of trying to get people to buy this thing. And to everybody else at Wisdom Publications for helping to bring this book into being. When I sent my manuscript to Wisdom I figured the best I'd get was the same "Dear Author: We didn't even bother to read your submission"-type form-letter I received from another well-known publisher of Buddhist books (who shall remain nameless) or the strange uncomprehending (and often incomprehensible) replies I got from mainstream publishers. But here I am, a Buddhist author at a Buddhist press. Who'da thunk it?

And, of course, thanks to my parents Dan and Sandy Warner for love and support and for providing me with an upbringing that allowed me to see a lot more of the world than most other kids from Wadsworth. Plus thanks to the rest of my family, particularly my grandpa Everett Warner, grandma Marian Warner and my aunt Sue who ruined her year of perfect high school attendance to see me as a baby. And, of course, my sister Stacey, her kids Ben and Skylar and their dad Dave. Ben and Sky, please ignore all the dirty words in here, okay?

Thanks as well to Tim McCarthy's teacher, Kobun Chino Otogawa, who I never got to meet, but whose wonderful translation of the Heart Sutra led to a major turning point in my life. Also thanks to his daughter Yoshiko Chino, his wife Katrin Otogawa, and his lawyer Hollis deLancy for allowing me to use it in this book.

Thanks also to the late Noboru Tsuburaya who gave me the opportunity to realize my dreams and, more importantly, to realize the true nature of such dreams. Thanks to his son Kazuo Tsuburaya for not getting rid of me in spite of all the times I've screwed things up for the company and to Masahiro Tsuburaya and Akira Tsuburaya for (hopefully) doing the same. And I can't forget Koichi Takano, whose special effects work I admired since I was five years old and who, for a while, I got to call "boss." Thanks, as well, to Jimmy Ugawa and Atsushi Saito for putting up with me all these years. After nearly ten years I'm still happy and proud I work for Tsuburaya Productions, the best producers of Japanese monster movies in the business. *Gabare ("Go!") Ultraman!*

And thank you Jimi Imij, Johnny Phlegm, Tommy Strange, and Mickey X-Nelson, the other members of Zero Defex (though John left before I joined) as well as Fraser Suicyde, Jim Krane, Mike Mohawk, Sue Hess, Dan Yell, Jimmy Dread, Sean "Trick Bunny" Saley, Sleazy Jesus, Dan Gaffney, Lesa the Death Lady, and everyone else who was there. We had a good time, huh? And to the other members of Dimentia 13, most importantly Joe Nlolflzlilglelr, my best friend since seventh grade who still likes to tell me how full of shit I am, and Louanne Lisk for soaring harmonies. Thanks as well to Dave Swanson who wasn't with Dimentia 13 long but who is the only drummer I've ever played with (other than Mickey) who really listened to what the rest of the band was doing. And I haven't forgotten J.D. Martignon of Midnight Records who gave me the chance to make records. When are those reissues due, J.D.? And thanks to Glenn Rhese of Plasticland who made the album *Disturb the Air* sound so huge. Thanks as well to Ira Robbins for giving Dimentia 13 more space than Nirvana in the Trouser Press Record Guide (okay, it was in 1991 and who knew? But still, thanks).

And what would my life have been like without the members of My Niece's Foot; Nick "Vic Wild Thing" Wilding, Sam "The Rock" Flemming, and Emily "The One Who Could Actually Sing" Iarocci plus our dedicated fan club Ginger and Anjali? Sorry you guys didn't get more space in this book. Next time, I promise. (In case you care, my rock 'n' roll nickname in the band was "Stu" after The Beatles' dead bass player.)

Also here's to the many people with whom I shared cheap living spaces during the "Prosperous Reagan Years" when I could hardly afford Top Ramen®: Logan Lestat, Laura Rachel, Steve McKee, Bill Ferrell, Lesa Lilly, Sue Cihla, Mary Bauch, Becky Wagner, Dale Houston (cuz you two were around a lot), and everyone else who put up with my noise and mess. And thanks to each and every high school and other related facility that turned down my applications for work during those years. Don't ever be disappointed with what happens in life because sometimes you don't know when someone is doing you a tremendous favor. Seriously.

Then there's everyone in Nishijima's group Dogen Sangha, particularly Taijun Saito, Peter Rocca, Harumi

Saito, Isamu Takenaka, Shin and Yumi Kiriki, Jeremy and
Reiko Pearson, and Mike and Yoko Leutchford. And special
thanks to everyone who did not walk out as soon as they
learned Nishijima was handing his weekly lectures over to
a know-nothing little punk like me.

Thanks to Dana Mitchell for patiently reading and cri-
tiquing my writing when no one else wanted to know. And
to Miki Mochizuki for listening to a lot of my rants that
eventually went into this book. Thanks to everyone who
reads my website (www.hardcorezen.org) for letting me test
out some of this stuff on you. When I wasn't making sense
you always told me so. Please keep it up.

Thanks as well to the bands who meant so much to me
when I was a young tyke (and not such a young tyke): The
Who, The Beatles, Syd Barrett, KISS®, The Sex Pistols, The
Ramones, Iggy and the Stooges, The Cramps, Black Flag,
Minor Threat, The Misfits, The Meat Puppets, The Dick-
ies, The Descendents, ALL, PiL, The Dead Kennedys,
MDC, Robyn Hitchcock, Teenage Fanclub, Flaming Lips,
and all the great Akron/Kent bands like Rubber City
Rebels, Starvation Army, The F-Models, Hammer-Damage,
Urban Mutants, and Bongo's Jungle Party.

Also thanks to anyone not mentioned or expecting to be
mentioned in these acknowledgments who's actually read
down this far. I never read the acknowledgments sections in
books. Boring, boring, boring. Who cares about all these
people you never heard of? So here's a joke as a reward for
sticking with me: *How many Zen masters does it take to
screw in a light bulb? The plum tree in the garden!* Haw!
Get it?

Finally a big huge thank you to my luscious wife, Yuka,
for never giving up.

If you liked HARDCORE ZEN, check out these:

BLUE JEAN BUDDHA

VOICES OF YOUNG BUDDHISTS

Edited by Sumi Loundon
Foreword by Jack Kornfield
288 pages, ISBN 0-861781-177-7, $16.95

"These stories are **NOT AT ALL WHAT YOU'RE USED TO HEARING.**"
—Angela Watrous, editor of Bare Your Soul: The Thinking Girl's Guide to Enlightenment

"This is **AN IDEA WHOSE TIME HAS COME.**" —Publishers Weekly

"**THESE 20- AND 30-SOMETHINGS REALLY GET IT,** in a way that perhaps their parents did not. They write of finding peace and practice in **NEW YORK CITY;** of taking vows of celibacy while continuing to be a **PUNK ROCKER.** They seek, investigate, **QUESTION,** retreat, sit zazen, or chant as part of their practice—the new American Buddhism. There is wisdom here for all ages." —NAPRA ReVIEW

"These stories **RESONATE.**" —Shambhala Sun

"Here are the voices of **YOUNGER PEOPLE** bringing their own **GENERATIONAL CONCERNS** and **CULTURAL SPIN** to the Buddha's teaching. Blue Jean Buddha is a testimony to the timelessness of the dharma, as well as to the vitality of a new generation that is taking it to heart." —Inquiring Mind

NOVICE TO MASTER

<u>AN ONGOING LESSON IN THE
EXTENT OF MY OWN STUPIDITY</u>

by Soko Morinaga

Translated by Belenda Attaway
Yamakawa

144 pages, ISBN 0-86171-393-1,
$11.95

"A spiritual autobiography by
an accomplished master of Zen,
and also A COMPELLING STORY OF COMING OF AGE in post-war
Japan. One can't help but be drawn to the genuine
tone of Morinaga's voice and his SENSE OF HUMOR."
—Shambhala Sun

"Soko Morinaga Roshi has TAKEN ME PLACES THAT MAPS CAN
ONLY HINT OF. This is one of the rarest books, among
but a handful of such truly wondrous books—words on
the order of Issa and Thoreau—the kind that changes
your mind and your eyes for the rest of your days."
—Bill Shields, author of The Southeast Asian Book of
the Dead

"UNPRETENTIOUS, POIGNANT AND INSIGHTFUL. Artfully written and
translated, Novice to Master weaves personal narrative
together with key concepts of Zen practices."
—Sumi Loundon, editor of Blue Jean Buddha

"If Novice to Master were just a monk's story, it
would be worth reading. But it is far more. It is
the story of A MAN'S DEVOTION TO GETTING IT—WHATEVER IT
MAY BE." —RALPH: The Review of Arts, Literature, Philosophy and the Humanities

HOW TO RAISE AN OX

ZEN PRACTICE AS TAUGHT IN MASTER DOGEN'S SHOBOGENZO

Francis Dojun Cook

Foreword by Taizan Maezumi Roshi

208 pages, ISBN 0-86171-317-6, $14.95

"An **OUTSTANDING** introduction to the most important Zen master in Japanese history. Francis Dojun Cook provides a brilliant translation of ten carefully selected chapters from **DOGEN'S MASTERPIECE, SHOBOGENZO.** These chapters are preceded by a series of short essays written by Cook, which distill the essence of what follows and provide an **IDEAL INTRODUCTION** to it. These essays help the reader to grasp the more subtle and elusive aspects of Dogen's **PROFOUND AND EXTRAORDINARILY CREATIVE WRITING.** Cook has a remarkable grasp of the heart of Dogen's thinking and a genius for communicating it." —Jeremy D. Safran, editor of Psychoanalysis and Buddhism

THE GREAT AWAKENING

A BUDDHIST SOCIAL THEORY

David R. Loy

320 pages, ISBN 0-86171-366-4, $16.95

"**I LOOK FOR DEEPER MEANING EVERYWHERE. LOY'S BOOK SURE GAVE ME SOME**—not only on that personal how-to-live-my-life level, but also in the universal realm of what's-this-all-about." —Kalle Lasn, editor-in-chief of Adbusters Magazine and author of Culture Jam: The Uncooling of America

ON ZEN PRACTICE
BODY, BREATH, AND MIND

Edited by Taizan Maezumi Roshi and Bernie Glassman

Foreword by Robert Aitken

208 pages, ISBN 0-86171-315-X, $16.95

Conceived as the essential ZEN PRIMER, this book ADDRESSES EVERY ASPECT OF ZEN PRACTICE: beginning practice, chanting, sesshin, shikantaza, working with Mu, the nature of koans, and more.

"A DAZZLING DISPLAY of wisdom about how to use spiritual practices to enlighten our EVERYDAY LIFE."
—Zen teachers Chozen and Hogen Bays, co-abbots of Great Vow Zen Monastery

THE ART OF JUST SITTING
ESSENTIAL WRITINGS ON THE ZEN PRACTICE OF SHIKANTAZA

Edited by John Daido Loori

Introduction by Taigen Dan Leighton

224 pages, 0-86171-327-3, $16.95

'Just sit' is one of the most COMMONLY HEARD—AND LEAST UNDERSTOOD—phrases associated with Zen Buddhism. Zen master John Daido Loori brings together teachings of some of the most prominent ANCIENT and MODERN teachers." —Tricycle

"For the first time, now gathered in one volume, we can read 1500 YEARS OF THE DISCOVERY OF THE TRUE PATH of discovery and realize what it means to be truly present for life as it is. A jewel of a book." —Joan Halifax Roshi, Head Teacher, Upaya Zen Center

"A COOL BOOK; it takes the risk of going deep." —John Tarrant, Zen teacher and Director of the Pacific Zen Institute

ABOUT WISDOM

WISDOM PUBLICATIONS, a nonprofit publisher, is dedicated to preserving and transmitting important works from all the major Buddhist traditions as well as related East-West themes.

To learn more about Wisdom, or browse our books on-line, visit our website at wisdompubs.org. You may request a copy of our mail-order catalog on-line or by writing to:

Wisdom Publications
199 Elm Street
Somerville, Massachusetts 02144 USA
Telephone: (617) 776-7416
Fax: (617) 776-7841
Email: info@wisdompubs.org
www.wisdompubs.org

The Wisdom Trust

As a nonprofit publisher, Wisdom is dedicated to the publication of fine Dharma books for the benefit of all sentient beings and dependent upon the kindness and generosity of sponsors in order to do so. If you would like to make a donation to Wisdom, please do so through our Somerville office. If you would like to sponsor the publication of a book, please write or email us at the address above.

Thank you.

Wisdom is a nonprofit, charitable 501(c)(3) organization affiliated with the Foundation for the Preservation of the Mahayana Tradition (FPMT).